The Zane Way to a Beautiful Body

FRANK AND CHRISTINE ZANE

Through Weight Training for Men and Women

PHOTOGRAPHS BY KENN DUNCAN

SIMON AND SCHUSTER · NEW YORK

COPYRIGHT © 1979 BY FRANK ZANE AND CHRISTINE ZANE
ALL RIGHTS RESERVED
INCLUDING THE RIGHT OF REPRODUCTION
IN WHOLE OR IN PART IN ANY FORM
PUBLISHED BY SIMON & SCHUSTER
A DIVISION OF GULF & WESTERN CORPORATION
SIMON & SCHUSTER BUILDING
ROCKEFELLER CENTER
1230 AVENUE OF THE AMERICAS
NEW YORK, NEW YORK 10020

DESIGNED BY EVE METZ
MANUFACTURED IN THE UNITED STATES OF AMERICA

3   4   5   6   7   8   9   10

LIBRARY OF CONGRESS CATALOGING IN PUBLICATION DATA

ZANE, FRANK.
    THE ZANE WAY TO A BEAUTIFUL BODY THROUGH WEIGHT TRAINING FOR MEN
AND WOMEN.
    1. BODYBUILDING.   2. EXERCISE.   I. ZANE, CHRISTINE, JOINT AUTHOR.
II. TITLE.
GV514.Z36   646.7'5   78–15653
ISBN 0-671-24367-5

ACKNOWLEDGMENTS

We would like to thank the following people who have helped us in ways too numerous to mention: Arnold Schwarzenegger; Bob Datilla; George Butler; Charles Gaines; Harry Schwartz; Rheo Blair; Joe Weider; William Como; Kenn Duncan; Tom Orr. And a very special acknowledgment to our parents.

We dedicate this book to each other.

Contents

Contents

Introduction

Our book is for men and women of all ages who want to improve their bodies. The information we provide is based on our personal experience of bodybuilding with and without weight-training apparatus. We use the word "bodybuilding" in the sense of "body creation" because you can do much more than just build up your body with this book; by following our instructions and suggestions you will be able to create a more beautiful body.

Even though men and women have the same muscles, the emphasis on how to develop these muscles will be quite different. For example, most women do not want to develop muscular arms and broad shoulders like a man's, but they do want a smaller waistline, a firmer bust, and shapely hips and thighs. Our book has separate sections for men and women in order to enable both men and women to improve in their own unique ways.

Most of the exercises can be performed using a minimum of equipment and can even be done at home. The programs for men start with a very basic bodybuilding routine which will develop the muscles without the use of weights, and are followed by programs which progress to three-, four-, five-, and six-day-a-week programs up to the level of twice-a-day training for the advanced bodybuilder who enters physique competition. There is a section on posing for the competitive bodybuilder, how to use bodybuilding apparatus found in a commercial gym or health studio, and other essentials of competitive bodybuilding such as "A Quick Muscle-size-building Program."

The women's programs will systematically take them through three progressive levels of free form exercises (without weights). This section is perfect for use either in group exercise classes or alone if you prefer. Following the free form exercise programs are the Basic, Middle, and Success weight-training routines, each one progressively more difficult and emphasizing different problem areas of the woman's body.

The exercises in all sections are interchangeable, and women can do movements listed in the men's section and vice versa, which makes our book an even more versatile tool for working with individual differences. Along with the exercises in the individual men's and women's sections, you can have a lot of fun doing the flexibility and muscle-toning exercises shown in the Exercises for Couples section, where you will exercise using resistance supplied by your partner. In all, we give complete descriptions of how to perform over 120 exercises, how the different areas of the body are worked by these exercises, and how to breathe correctly while doing each movement. The book is completely illustrated, with over 200 photographs of movements performed by the authors.

Bodybuilding and physical fitness are not all a matter of exercise, so we give advice on sensible nutrition as well: the function of different classes of foods, vitamins, and minerals; diets for gaining or losing weight gradually; how to use a food journal to improve your eating habits. We also emphasize the psychological side of developing a beautiful body, with instruction on mental preparation before exercise through the use of imagery; a technique for improving concentration by training your span of attention; and a total relaxation method to use following your workout. You'll learn how to set physical goals, and how to monitor and evaluate your progress by using graphs, tape measurements, the mirror, and the Workout Journal.

The Zane Way to a Beautiful Body can easily be adapted for use as a text to teach bodybuilding in health studios, schools, camps, and colleges. We use it as a teaching tool in the many bodybuilding seminars we conduct across the country. The fact that both sexes of any age can use our book together or separately makes it the perfect family physical-fitness book as well. With it, a man and a woman can progress together because both are actively involved in a positive physical relationship.

We have used the programs we recommend in this book, and they have been of great benefit to us in our desire for self-improvement and physical well-being. Additionally, our common interest in bodybuilding has brought us closer together and deepened our feelings and commitment toward each other. We have come to realize that we have a responsibility to look good and be fit not only for ourselves but also for each other. In the words of A. R. Orage:

> To be in love demands that the lover shall divine the wishes of the beloved long before they have come into the beloved's own consciousness. He knows her better than she knows herself; and loves her more than she loves herself; so that she becomes her perfect self without her own conscious effort. Her conscious effort, when the love is mutual, is for him. Thus each delightfully works perfection in the other.*

If you have someone for whom you want to look good, our book is for you. You owe it to yourself and you owe it to the other person.

ABOUT THE AUTHORS

Frank grew up in a tough Pennsylvania coal-mining town. He was always quiet and shy when he was young but often found himself trying to finish a fight which his brother had started, only to get beat up. He discovered bodybuilding at about this time, when he was fourteen years old. He walked into one of his classes in junior high school and spotted a muscle-building magazine in the wastebasket. He studied the magazine and started training soon thereafter at the weight room of the Wilkes-Barre YMCA. He also bought a 30-pound set of dumbbells and trained at home. His parents were angry at him for devoting time to training when they felt he should be doing work around the house. "Build yourself up by cutting the grass," they would tell him. This only made Frank all the more determined to succeed. Frank worked out with weights for three years in high school, with two four-month lapses during football season. He developed from 130 pounds at age fourteen to 160 pounds at age seventeen. He was very serious about

---

* A. R. Orage. *On Love*. New York: Samuel Weiser.

bodybuilding and felt great because he could actually see the results he was getting.

While in high school Frank spent his summers as an archery instructor at a summer camp. He would hitchhike home 20 miles on weekends. Since he had no weights at home (they were all at camp) he'd carry 50 pounds of weights along with him so he could train! He made sure never to miss a workout. His parents' attitude about bodybuilding began changing as they realized his dedication. Frank's mother especially encouraged him in his training.

Frank graduated first in his high school class and won his first two trophies ever—for academic achievement. He attended nearby Wilkes College, from which he received a B.S. in secondary education in 1964. All this time he continued to train, and he began entering physique competition. His trophy collection had grown and so had he. He had won over two dozen trophies and now weighed 185 pounds! Frank spent two years teaching and training in Pennsylvania and New Jersey before he moved to Florida in 1966. He was very serious about competitive training. He was winning every contest around and now felt he was destined for bigger things. Frank wanted to move to California, but it would mean severing a lot of East Coast ties, and he wasn't ready for that, so he moved to Florida instead.

In the meantime Christine was growing up in Florida with her three sisters. They were a close family, and children and parents did a lot of outdoor activities such as swimming and boating on the Gulf Coast and Sunday picnics and outings with the family. There was hardly a day she did not spend in the warm tropical Florida sunshine playing and soaking up the sun.

Christine was born with a natural artistic talent for drawing and painting. She had entered many local art contests as a child and had won recognition for her talents. In her high school years she began selling some of her paintings, usually to friends and acquaintances. Her artistic talents seemed to come from her father, who did everything he could to encourage and inspire her.

Christine became very popular in high school. She always maintained a B average, but liked to socialize more than study. She became active in civic organizations and was head pep-squad leader, marching in parades and at football games.

When Frank and Christine met in Florida in September 1966 she had just begun junior college and he was teaching at a local junior high where Christine's little sister was a student. Her little sister thought it would be a good idea to have a bodybuilding champion for a brother-in-law and decided to ask Frank home to meet her sister, Christine.

Frank had been bodybuilding for almost ten years before he moved to Florida in search of a better climate and training conditions. When Christine met Frank, this was her first encounter with anyone who had developed his body so completely. She had seen all of the Hercules movies when she was younger but had just assumed these men grew that way naturally. She soon learned otherwise and took up bodybuilding as a means to improve her own figure. She had always had a fairly good figure but found it very difficult to keep her weight under control. With weight training, she found her weight easier to control and she felt a lot more energetic from her daily training sessions.

Frank was training for the Mr. America contest and Christine became interested in competing for beauty titles. She won all of the local competitions she entered in Florida and then decided to compete for the Miss Americana crown in New York City in 1967. Frank had initially shown Christine how he trained and what kind of results bodybuilding exercises produced. Christine then took what Frank had shown her and modified it into a program that gave her the type of figure she wanted to develop. It worked! Christine won her contest, but Frank came in second in his.

They were married a few months later. Frank continued teaching junior high school mathematics and Christine managed a nearby women's health studio. They both continued bodybuilding: Christine exercised hard to set an example for the women in the studio and Frank started serious training for the 1968 Mr. America competition, which he won. One week after winning the Mr. America title, Frank defeated Arnold Schwarzenegger for the Mr. Universe title in Miami.

Several months later the Zanes moved to California. Frank began teaching mathematics in Los Angeles while Christine went to college and taught women's exercise classes in Santa Monica. Since moving to California, Frank won the Mr. World title in 1969, the Mr. Universe title in 1970 and 1972, as well as in 1968, and the coveted Mr. Olympia title (world professional bodybuilding champion) in 1977 after 21 years of training. He also earned a second bachelor's degree in psychology. Christine won the Miss Universe Bikini Crown in 1970 and then retired from competition to devote her time to her studies and her art. She graduated from college with high honors and a B.A. in art and then went on to get her teaching credentials and obtained a teaching position in Santa Monica. During her years of teaching she spent her evenings and summers attending California State University where she earned a Masters Degree in the Fine Arts. Much of Christine's spare time is spent creating surrealistic pencil drawings and paintings.

PART I

A Healthy Body

1 · Similarities and Differences in Men's and Women's Training

Two terms that you will need to know the meaning of are repetitions, or reps, and sets. A repetition is one complete movement within each exercise. A set is a specified number of repetitions done consecutively.

Both men and women have the same muscles, but naturally they don't want to develop them the same way. Actually no one has to worry about developing big muscles. For muscles to grow large, a lot of hard and heavy training is needed—it doesn't happen by accident.

Should men and women follow the same exercise programs? It all depends on what you want to look like. Women don't want big arms, so they wouldn't do much arm work except what's needed for firming. Also, women would use less weight on their exercises than men because heavy weights build muscle size. Both men and women should always do each set of every exercise with the intention of getting a "pump" on every set. A pump is a physical sensation of blood "pumping" into the muscles being exercised. Results will come much faster when you get a pump on each set.

There are three basic conditions that determine how much of a pump you'll get: 1. Make sure you use a weight heavy enough to permit you to do the exact number of repetitions you are to do for each set in good form. Rest between sets only as long as it takes for breathing to return to normal. (This is usually between one-half and three minutes between sets, depending on which muscles you are working.) 2. When you are doing an exercise, you should watch yourself in a mirror or have a mental picture of yourself doing the exercise correctly. You should also mentally be counting the reps and feeling the pump coming on. 3. About one hour before you train you should have an easily digestible meal, consisting mostly of protein with some carbohydrate and fat. Then you should relax and thereby allow your blood sugar to build up. Then, when you train and get a pump, the blood that rushes to aid the muscle is carrying fuel (in this case a substantial amount of blood sugar). Training when you are very hungry is a mistake. But don't overeat either. If you have meat or fish before training, eat it slowly and in small amounts because meats, fish and poultry take longer to digest than eggs or dairy products.

In general, doing six to eight reps builds size to the muscles; ten reps develop a combination of size and muscularity; 12 to 15 reps develop muscular definition. A muscle shows good definition when you can see striations in it. This means there is very little subcutaneous fat between muscle and skin, so the muscles stand out prominently. Most women do not wish to become muscular through weight training; but they need not worry about this, because female hormones usually prevent this from happening. However, it is possible for a woman to get more muscular if she trains like a man and deliberately uses heavy weights.

Women should always keep repetitions above eight on weight-training movements. (Some of the exercises for women in this book involve less than eight reps, but these are mostly for beginners getting accustomed to the exercise.) By training in this manner a woman can develop a more streamlined figure—building up those areas that need more development (bust measurement for example), firming flabby areas (such as back of arms), or slimming and shaping certain areas (thighs, waist, hips) with lighter weights and higher repetitions. In the women's training fewer weight exercises are recommended and more free-form exercises recommended than in men's training. This is because the emphasis in women's training is on graceful movements and stretching exercises for the leaner look. We do not train together except for the couples' exercise program, which we usually do when we are traveling and no exercise facilities are available. It's always good to have a training partner whenever possible; you should choose someone whose physical needs are similar to yours. Men's and women's bodies naturally are different, and so both men and women need to emphasize different areas in their workouts.

THE IDEAL WOMAN'S PHYSIQUE

We consider the ideal woman's figure to be: Entire body devoid of excess fat or flab; good muscle tone, yet an appearance of softness—nicely shaped muscles firm but not muscular looking; thighs slender with a slight sweep to the front and backs of thighs; well-rounded buttocks with hips measuring same size approximately as bust. Lower legs not straight up and down but with shapely calves; trim waistline with a slight taper to the upper back; well-developed bust, slim arms and straight shoulders with good posture and slim neck.

THE IDEAL MAN'S PHYSIQUE

The ideal man's physique should show: broad, well-developed shoulders with a strong-looking neck (but not too large); chest (pectoral) muscles with upper and outer sections fully developed, creating a squared-off look but not too large; back with good muscularity and a nice taper to a small muscular waist; well-developed upper arms and forearms; small hips and streamlined thighs with good separation to the frontal thigh; and well-developed leg biceps and full, well-rounded calf development.

The key words to developing a man's or woman's physique are symmetry and proportion. Every part of the body should be in balance with every other part. If you have any areas that develop easier than other areas, don't work these areas so hard, and do more work for your weak points. Learn what your weak points are—try to notice them when looking into the mirror and listen to objective criticism from others. You can improve these underdeveloped areas by following the programs in this book. A good way to set up your program is to exercise your weak points first in your routine. This way you'll pay more attention to them and work them harder, since your energy level is always higher at the beginning of your workout.

2 · How to Exercise Successfully

BREATHING

Each exercise is accompanied by instructions on breathing techniques for that specific movement. Follow these instructions exactly. At first you may have to spend a bit of time learning to breathe correctly, but the results will give you more stamina and strength during the movements. Breathing correctly will also help your timing on each repetition and your pace will be better. In general, you inhale as you begin each repetition at the beginning of the movement, and you exhale as you finish each repetition at the end of the movement. Do not hold your breath after you inhale but begin exhaling slowly as you complete each repetition.

MOVEMENTS

The actual movement of an exercise is very important. Do the movements slowly, using light weights at first. As your strength increases and you begin to use heavier weights, you can increase the speed of each repetition. The movement should always be correct, with little or no cheating. Cheating is not using correct form in an exercise. In weight training, cheating enables a bodybuilder to handle more weight, but he or she does so at the expense of working other muscles than those intended. Poor muscle shape often results from cheating even though the muscles may grow larger.

THE BODY THRIVES ON ROUTINE

Be sure to set aside the same time period to practice your exercises each day. With Frank this time is 10 A.M. to noon. Christine usually trains from 1 P.M. to 2 P.M. Choose the hours that are most compatible with your job and your lifestyle. Early-morning training has its advantages: the mind is usually more relaxed early in the morning and you get a good feeling from completing your training early. But it also has its disadvantages: sleepiness from getting up early, occasional weakness from not being awake long enough and not eating enough meals to keep the blood sugar up. We find that we are strongest between 10 A.M. and 4 P.M. each day. Any earlier or later and we are not up to par physically.

In our book you will find exercise routines or programs. Choose the one most practical for you. The body thrives on routine. Exercises done haphazardly without a plan or program result in little physical gain. Follow each program as directed the same time each day you train.

Within each of the programs recommendations are made that allow for age differences: *young people* ages twelve to twenty; *adults* ages twenty-one to forty; and *older people* over forty. These age groupings are only approximate and may vary with each person because of individual differences in heredity, health, and psychological factors. The programs are also arranged by levels of difficulty: *beginners* having no previous exercise experience in the past few months; *intermediates* who have been exercising mildly twice a week or so; and *advanced* students who have been doing weight training or free-form exercises regularly and are in fairly good condition. Some routines place emphasis on different areas and are described before each routine.

It is a good idea to begin at the beginners' level for at least one week whenever you start a new routine. After this you can gradually increase sets, reps and weights as you get in better shape and progress to intermediate and advanced levels. The day after exercising you may feel a slight soreness in those areas you exercised. This is normal and shows these areas are responding to the exercise. However, if the soreness is severe, you are doing too much and must cut back on sets and/or weights in your program. A good way to help alleviate muscular soreness is to exercise those sore areas with light weights and high repetitions several days in succession to bring a fresh blood supply into the area. In this way you can work the muscular soreness out in less time than it would normally take the soreness to disappear if you did nothing for it.

Your routine is arranged in a definite pattern. Follow it, paying attention to the suggestions as well as to the photos of the movement. Establish a rhythm in your training and follow it throughout your workout. You will need rest periods between each set. Do not rest longer than it takes your breathing to return to normal. During this rest period prepare your mind and body for the next exercise or movement. Don't lose your concentration through idle conversation or trying to do unrelated tasks during the rest period. Once you have begun your routine, keep your mind and body directed toward your training.

Each time you exercise, begin the session with a mental-preparation exercise. This is important in establishing the right atmosphere and attitude for your workout. Next come your warm-up movements, which prepare the body by increasing circulation, allowing greater flexibility, and preventing injury to the muscles. These warm-ups also begin working specific muscle groups, depending on the warm-up being done. Then you will begin your workout. As mentioned previously, your weak areas should be exercised first because your energy level is always highest at the beginning of your workout, and so you will put more into improving this area. When you do the exercises for each body part one after the other you keep more blood in this area and work the muscle more directly. Notice that the waist is never worked first but usually close to or at the end of the routine when the stomach is emptiest. At the end of each routine there is a relaxation exercise. After a period of intense exercise you will need this to help you relax tense muscles and prepare yourself for the rest of the day.

You Create Your Body

There is no simple way to get physically fit. You must put out some energy to get results. A machine can't do it for you, nor can wraps, massages, or gadgets. You are the only one who can get yourself into better shape and improve the appearance of your body. If your body is out of proportion a diet alone will not remedy this problem. Dieting alone may cause you to lose where you already are slim, and you'll only appear as a smaller version of your former self. Yet combine exercise and diet and you will see yourself creating an entirely new body. Regular exercising will enable you to have more control over where you lose and where you gain. But exercise alone won't work: you must follow a sensible, well-balanced diet as well.

Whether you realize it or not, you create your own body. There are two categories of body creation, and most people fall into the *unconscious creation* category. They are unaware of their bodies and what they are doing to them. They eat junk foods and get very little or no regular exercise. As they grow older their bodies gradually deteriorate and look worse and worse. Their metabolism slows down and they gain weight by accumulating more body fat. Physiologists tell us that after the late twenties most people's bodies start going downhill. In bodybuilding, we've seen men and women in their forties in the best shape of their lives. So it's really not too late to get into good shape right now, no matter how old you are. Improvement is possible at any age. But first you must realize that you created your body as it is now and you are responsible for your appearance and health. You have been causing changes in your body all along—negative changes that have worked against your appearance and health. Once you realize that you, and nobody else, caused your body to be the way it is right now, then *conscious creation* of the body becomes possible.

The body is never static; it is always changing. When you live in a way that nourishes your body, you can make your body look as you wish. You don't have to get out of shape as you grow older—you should be in better shape because you have accumulated more years of conscious body creation. The secret is; after you get into reasonably good shape, don't allow yourself to get out of shape. If you must stop training, it is better to allow your body weight to drop by eating less than you did when you were exercising.

If you were exercising regularly years ago, have taken a few years' layoff, and again begin to work out, you will find that the development that you once achieved will gradually return until your body is again in good condition. It seems that the muscle cells have a memory, and once you achieve a certain physical development you can usually regain or even improve on it, providing you work hard enough and haven't let yourself go too far in the wrong direction.

MENTAL PREPARATION

Each time before you begin your exercises, prepare yourself mentally. This mental-preparation exercise will help you to relax as well as to visualize more clearly exactly what you want to do with your body. When you visualize your routine and how the movements are done before they are actually performed, they seem to be done with more success and ease when you train.

Find a place where you can concentrate and relax. It is preferable to do this mental exercise in the area where you are going to train. However, this may not be possible if you train away from home. So plan to do your mental preparation just prior to leaving for the gym, if that is where you train.

It may be easier and more relaxing if you record these instructions on a cassette and play them softly before each workout session. This way you don't have to bother with reading or memorizing.

Sit down or lie on your back with arms at sides and legs straight. Close your eyes. Begin to breathe deeply through your nostrils. Inhale very deeply, expanding the lungs to their fullest, and exhale completely. As you exhale, each time allow your body to relax a little bit more. Relax your entire body as you feel yourself breathing, staying aware of your body completely. Beginning with your toes, totally relax toes, feet and ankles. Remove all tension from the calves and knees, continuing to breathe fully and completely. Move your awareness up to your thighs and hips. Completely relax this area. Let your abdomen and buttocks relax. Breathing very deeply, allow your chest and back to relax. Notice all of the tension now disappearing from your neck. Breathe deeply and relax all your facial muscles. Let go the tightness in your lips, eyes and forehead. Take a very deep breath and notice that your entire body is now relaxed. If any area is holding tension, return to this area and dissolve the tension. Feel it being lifted out of your body. Now bring an image of yourself into your mind. See yourself doing your routine step by step. You see yourself doing the movements easily and gracefully. Each movement is in perfect form. Follow through to the end of the routine. Now bring an image of yourself into mind. See yourself in fantastic shape, looking as you wish to look when your goal is met. You feel extremely radiant, happy and energetic. Stretch your body. Open your eyes slowly. You are now ready to begin exercising.

RELAXATION

After each exercise session it is very important to relax your body completely. By doing so you will be allowing the muscles to unstress (tension stored in the muscles is released in this manner; unstressing comes in the form of seemingly involuntary muscle twitches). After your relaxation period your mind will be much clearer and your body more relaxed.

As we suggested with the mental preparation, it may prove easier for you if you record these instructions on a tape which can be played after you finish your exercise routine. To begin, lie flat on your back, palms facing upward, and your feet approximately 18 inches apart. Take deep breaths. Concentrate on your lungs as they expand and contract. Close your eyes and continue breathing deeper and deeper. Inhale until your lungs are completely filled and exhale until you have expelled all the air from your lungs. Focus your attention on your feet. Flex them, curl your toes, and roll your ankles in all directions. Now allow your feet to rest and relax completely. Begin tensing and then relaxing your legs and knees. Flex and relax your legs three times. Each time you flex and relax your legs they become more and more relaxed. Begin tensing your buttocks and abdomen; tense and relax. Continue to breathe very deeply, relaxing more and more with each breath. Now tense and then relax your hip area. Begin tensing and relaxing your back and chest. Breathe deeply and relax this area completely. Next, tense and relax your arms. Stretch your fingers and totally relax your hands. Now tighten your neck and facial muscles. Take a deep breath and completely relax these muscles. Slowly direct your attention throughout your entire body. Are there any areas still holding tension? If so, take a deep breath, pulling the tension out of the muscles and exhale it out of your body completely. Mentally move through your body again. Notice how completely relaxed you are. Let your body become very heavy, as if you were dissolving and melting into the floor. You are now totally relaxed and completely free of tension.

Let your breathing continue to be deep and relaxed. Bring a vision of yourself into your mind. Become familiar with exactly how your body looks. Now gradually begin changing your image of yourself until you see yourself as you would like to look. Get to know this ideal image. Study it carefully and become familiar with it. If there are any changes you'd like to make in your image do so mentally until you are completely satisfied. Go into extreme detail with your visual description. Keep this image in your mind and feel your body becoming lighter. See yourself floating in midair, completely free from tension. Create a peaceful space around your floating body. Maybe you are floating over a sunny meadow of spring flowers. The sky is clear blue and filled with fluffy white clouds. Create the environment which is most peaceful and pleasing to you. Allow it to change whenever and however you wish. R–E–E–E–L–A–A–A–A–A–A–X. Slowly come out of this deep relaxation by inhaling deeply as you raise and stretch your arms overhead, at the same time stretching your legs and feet. Now exhale as you bring your arms back to rest near your sides. You will feel very happy, energetic, and looking better than ever as you slowly open your eyes. Get up when you feel ready and begin your normal daily activities.

GRESS CHART AND GRAPH

find it easier to continue with a program of ex-
ition when they begin to see concrete evidence of

Muscles of the Body

NAME	LOCATION	MOVEMENT
Trapezius	Upper back and each side of neck	Shoulder-shrugging and upward-pulling movements
Deltoids	Shoulders	Arm raising and overhead pressing
Pectorals	Chest	Horizontal pressing and drawing arms across body
Latissimus Dorsi	Wide back muscle stretching over back up to rear Deltoids	Pulling and rowing movements
Serratus	Jagged sawtooth muscles between Pectorals and Latissimus Dorsi	Pullover and Serratus leverage movements
Spinal Erectors	Lower length of spinal column	Raising upper body from a bent-over position
Biceps	Front portion of upper arm	Arm bending and twisting
Forearms	Between wrist and elbow	Reverse-grip arm bending
Triceps	Back of upper arm	Pushing and straightening movements of upper arms
Rectus Abdominals	Muscular area between sternum and pelvis	Sit-up, leg-raising, knee-in movements
Intercostals	Sides of waist, running diagonally to Serratus	Waist twisting
External Oblique Abdominals	Lower sides of waist	Waist twisting and bending
Buttocks	Muscular area covering seat	Lunging, stooping, leg raising
Leg Biceps	Back of thighs	Raising lower leg to buttocks, bending forward and str... ing
Frontal Thighs	Front of thigh	Extending...
Calves	Lower leg between ankle and knee	Ra...

progress. Yet it is easy to forget what progress we've made, especially if we find ourselves at a sticking point. This is why we recommend keeping a progress chart on your measurements and goals, which you should check every 6 weeks, and a graph of your weight, which should be checked daily. Keeping these charts lets you see realistically what progress you are making. Of course your mirror is one of your best progress indicators. It should be used daily for critical analysis.

On the progress chart (the Personal Record sheet on page 35) you will find a place for all your body measurements. Take your measurements before eating and exercising. You will measure again in 6 weeks; this should be done at the same time of day you first took your measurements. After your second measuring session, you should look for areas of your body that you want to concentrate on in the future. Be aware of changes that occur, and don't be discouraged if at first you should gain slightly in areas you had thought you should lose, or vice versa. Muscles sometimes initially increase in size as they begin to firm up; this is no cause for undue concern. This effect will start reversing itself as you get into better shape. The scales can also be deceiving when you first get into an exercise program. As muscles begin to develop and body fat starts to diminish, you may find your weight increasing slightly at first because muscle tissue is denser than fat. Since an equal volume of muscle is heavier, it takes up less space than fat. Therefore you may be slimmer, yet weigh a little more. In the long run your appearance is what matters most. How you look is much more important than how much you weigh or how you measure by the tape.

On the progress chart you will find a space to set your goals. It is very important that you write down on paper exactly what you want to do with your body. Read your goals daily before your training session. Visualize what you have written. In this way you will find your goal more easily attainable. Everything you do should be directed toward his goal. Write down in detail exactly how you want to look and feel. six weeks you may have reached your goal and wish to set a new Fine! We recommend that you keep your goals small at first. This ey are more easily reached and your efforts are reinforced by you a sense of progress and reward. This reward or pat on the

33

WEIGHT GRAPH

Christine's Personal Weight Graph over a Period of 40 Days

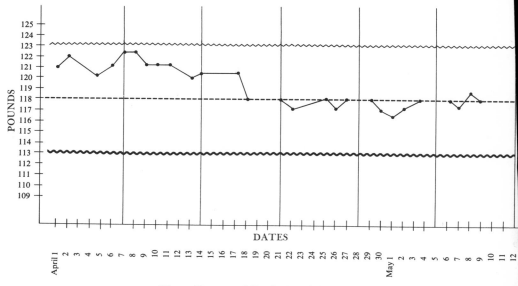

Your Personal Body Weight Graph

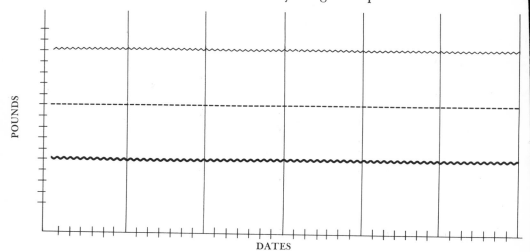

Personal Record

Be sure all information is accurate. Measure and weigh at the same time of day each occasion you do so, preferably before exercising or eating.

TODAY'S DATE_____HEIGHT _____WEIGHT_____
              month day year

How do you feel about your body today? _____

_____

_____

Measurements:

A. upper arm_____

B. upper chest_____

C. bustline_____

D. midriff_____

E. waistline _____

F. upper hips_____

G. hips and buttocks _____

H. right thigh _____

I. left thigh_____

J. right calf_____

K. left calf_____

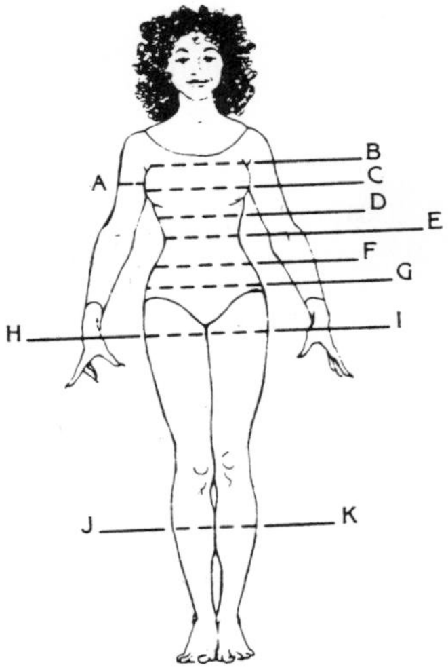

Goals: What progress would you like to make with your body? _____

_____

_____

Comments: _____

_____

_____

back for accomplishment is something we all need to keep us going.

Using a graph to keep track of your body weight is an effective method for giving you an idea of how you are progressing toward your goal. On this graph (Weight Graph page 34) locate your present body weight on the vertical scale and draw a horizontal broken line. If you need to lose weight, draw a wavy line no lower than ten pounds below the broken line. (After you lose this weight make a new graph.) Draw a zigzag line five pounds above your present weight. The area between the broken and the zigzag line is your danger zone. Use positive reinforcement by rewarding yourself (don't use food as a reward) every time your weight drops on your graph. Smaller-sized articles of clothing and events that help you physically are especially appropriate.

For gaining weight the procedure is reversed, with the wavy line no higher than a point ten pounds above your present weight. (When you achieve your goal make a new graph.) Your zigzag line will be at a point five pounds below your present weight, represented by the broken line. By rewarding yourself as you show progress you will keep your motivation high, and your progress is more likely to continue in the future.

Physical Checkup

One final bit of advice before you get started on your program. Get a complete physical examination from your physician and make sure there is nothing physically wrong with you before you begin your program. It is a good idea to have a complete physical examination at least once a year.

PART II

Bodybuilding for Men

3 · Bodybuilding without Weights: Basic Program I

If you've never trained with weights before, it would be a good idea to start your exercise program with Basic Program I, which involves no weights and very little equipment. This program should be followed 3 days per week and it works all the major muscle groups of the body. The only equipment required is 3 chairs or boxes, a broomstick, pole or bar, a doorway and a doorknob, and a calf block.* The program can be followed by men of any age, and it is a very handy way to keep in shape when you are traveling. For best results rest no longer than 1 minute between each set.

BODYBUILDING WITHOUT WEIGHTS
BASIC PROGRAM I

EXERCISE/PAGE	BEGINNER		INTERMEDIATE		ADVANCED	
	sets	reps	sets	reps	sets	reps
Mental Preparation						
Incline Push-ups 39	1	10	2	12	2	15
Push-ups with Feet Elevated 40	1	10	2	10	3	10
Wide-grip Broomstick Chins 41	1	10	2	10	3	10
Reverse Dips 42	1	10	2	10	3	10
Doorway Isometrics 43	1		2		3	
Doorknob Isometrics 44	1		2		3	
Free Squat 45	1	10	2	10	3	10
Two-legged Calf Raise 46	1	15	2	20	3	25
Leg Raise 47	1	15	2	20	3	25
Relaxation						

* The calf block is used for calf raises and enables you to get a full stretch all the way down by letting the heel descend below parallel position. To make a calf block simply fasten two 8-inch pieces of 2″-by-4″ lumber to an 18-inch piece of 2″-by-4″ with woodscrews or nails.

Train at the beginner's routine for at least one or two weeks before progressing to the intermediate routine. The same holds true for the intermediate routine. Train at the advanced routine for as long as you feel you are getting results from it. After it becomes too easy for you, move on to Basic Program II and follow the same progression. Your body should tell you when and how fast to progress. Learn to listen to it.

Special note:
All exercise descriptions which follow tell how to do one perfect repetition. Be sure to do each rep in every set this way.

INCLINE PUSH-UPS
Purpose: This exercise is easier than push-ups because of the angle. It should be done in place of push-ups if push-ups prove too hard. As you build strength, place feet on something higher, like a chair—this makes the exercise more difficult. This exercise works chest, triceps, and frontal deltoid muscles.

Equipment: Two chairs or boxes

Procedure: 1. Place two chairs or boxes 18 inches, or shoulder width, apart with backs against a wall so chairs won't move. 2. Place hands on front edge of chairs and feet about 4 feet away. Keep arms and legs straight. 3. Inhale and lower your upper body between the chairs by bending your arms and pivoting on your toes. 4. Push up when you reach bottom. You should feel a stretch in the chest area. Exhale as you return to starting position.

PUSH-UPS WITH FEET ELEVATED

Purpose: To develop the muscles of the chest, frontal deltoids and triceps. If this movement is too difficult, don't elevate your feet; simply do regular push-ups.

Equipment: One chair or chair-height box

Procedure: 1. Go down on hands and knees with hands shoulder-width apart. 2. Balancing on hands, elevate feet on a chair behind you. 3. Straighten body, inhale, bend arms and touch your chin to the floor. 4. Push yourself up by straightening your arms. 5. Exhale as you come to finish position. You should feel a pump mainly in the chest.

WIDE-GRIP BROOMSTICK CHINS

Purpose: This exercise works the upper back or latissimus dorsi muscles. These muscles when fully developed give the upper body a V taper. As your strength increases and the repetitions become easier, try to do regular chinups on an overhead bar with wide grip (see page 68).

Equipment: Two chairs or chair-height boxes and a five-foot pole or broomstick.

Procedure: 1. Place two chairs about three feet apart with backs facing each other. 2. Place pole over backs of chairs or tops of boxes. 3. Sit between chairs or boxes and grab pole with overhand grip, hands about three feet apart. 4. Straighten body so that only heels touch floor, inhale, and pull yourself up until chin touches pole. 5. Exhale as you lower to starting position. To build strength, lower yourself very slowly.

REVERSE DIPS

Purpose: This is one of the best, most direct exercises for triceps and shoulders. After a set of this movement the triceps should be really pumped.

Equipment: Three chairs or boxes

Procedure: 1. Place two chairs about 18 inches apart and the third chair about three feet away. 2. Squat between the two chairs and put one hand flat on the top of each of these with fingers pointing forward. 3. Put feet on third chair (heels resting on chair). 4. Inhale and dip between the two chairs as low as possible by bending arms. 5. When bottom is reached, start ascending by slowly straightening the arms. Exhale as you ascend.

DOORWAY ISOMETRICS

Purpose: This is an isometric exercise. You contract the shoulder muscles by resisting against an immovable object. This double movement is great for developing and building strength in the shoulders.

Equipment: An open doorway

Procedure: 1. Stand in middle of doorway and hold arms out to sides, pressing outside of forearms (right below elbows) against doorway. 2. Inhale and press arms against doorway trying to raise them. 3. Press arms as hard as you can for a slow count of ten and then exhale. 4. Relax for a count of ten. 5. Press hands against top of doorway (elbows should not be locked out and arms should be slightly bent). 6. Inhale and press upward as hard as you can for a count of ten. Exhale.

DOORKNOB ISOMETRICS

Purpose: Doorknobs make a good gripping device to do isometric curls, which strengthen the biceps and forearms.

Equipment: A double doorknob fastened to an open door

Procedure: 1. Place each foot on each side of an open door. 2. Grasp both knobs of the doorknob with a thumbless grip. The arms and knees should be slightly bent. 3. Inhale and imagine you are raising the doorknob upward in an arc or curling motion. Try to do this. 4. Hold for a slow count of ten. Exhale. 5. Feel the blood rushing into the biceps and forearm areas.

FREE SQUAT

Purpose: When done correctly this is a very good **exercise** for developing the thighs. Bodybuilders have done this exercise for years because it is a very effective shaping movement and no weight is needed.

Equipment: A 2″ x 4″ block to put under heels

Procedure: 1. Stand with heels 12 inches apart on block. Toes should point slightly outward. 2. Place hands on hips or hold onto something for support. 3. Contract the buttocks, keeping back straight, inhale, and squat to low position. 4. As you start to ascend, thrust hips forward and keep them forward until you reach finish position (exhale as you ascend). 5. Stop the upward movement when knees are slightly bent. You should feel a fantastic pump in the thighs.

TWO-LEGGED CALF RAISE

Purpose: This is the most basic exercise for developing the calf. Be sure to stand with toes on a calf block or a step so you can descend low with heels and rise way up on toes with each rep. High repetitions (15 to 25) are necessary to get a good pump. Do each rep slowly.

Equipment: A calf block (see page 38) or step and something to hold on to

Procedure: 1. Stand on a calf block with toes pointing straight ahead and feet about 12 inches apart. 2. Holding onto something to steady yourself, inhale and lower your heels as far as you can go. 3. Then ascend on toes by raising heels as far up as possible. Exhale.

LEG RAISE

Purpose: This is a very good movement for the abdominals, especially the lower section.

Equipment: Flat bench or floor

Procedure: 1. Lie on back on flat bench or floor with hands under hips (or holding on to bench, whichever is more comfortable), and feet together. 2. Inhale and slowly raise legs (keeping knees bent very slightly throughout the whole movement) until legs form a 45-degree angle with the floor. 3. Lower legs slowly until they are almost parallel to floor (exhale as you lower them).

4 · Bodybuilding with Weights: Basic Program II

The most common age for beginning bodybuilding seems to be the early teens. Bodybuilding apparently fits in with adolescent needs. The adolescent is looking for an identity and wants to be noticed and respected by his peers. Bodybuilding at this age is a great way to build self-confidence. When your body starts to develop you really feel good about yourself. Here is a good overall program that beginners can follow whether they are teen-agers, adults or older people. It is done three times a week: Monday, Wednesday, Friday, or Tuesday, Thursday, Saturday. It is a basic routine with 12 exercises that will build muscle if followed correctly. Stay at the beginner's level for one to two weeks, the intermediate level two to three weeks, and the advanced level at least one month before you go on to program III, the basic split routine. The weights suggested are only approximate poundages and the weights chosen may vary greatly with different individuals. Just remember to use a weight appropriate for the designated repetitions. If you use too light a weight the muscles will not be stimulated enough and will not respond. If you use too heavy a weight you may sustain an injury, and injuries are no fun. So it is really up to you to determine what your exercise poundages should be. Also, as you continue to train with weights, you should get stronger, and as you do, you should increase your training poundages. A method I really like to use in my training is to increase the weight on each successive set I do of each exercise. My first set is the lightest and serves as a warm-up. On barbell movement I add approximately 10 to 20 pounds each set and on dumbbell movements I usually jump about five pounds each set. In this way I can continually progress in my training poundages. Heavier weights build more size to the muscles. Lighter weights tone and condition the muscles. Keeping this in mind will help you to develop the kind of body you want.

BODYBUILDING WITH WEIGHTS
BASIC PROGRAM II

EXERCISE/PAGE	BEGINNER			INTERMEDIATE			ADVANCED		
	sets	reps	weight	sets	reps	weight	sets	reps	weight
Mental Preparation									
Press Behind Neck 50	1	10	50	2	10	75	3	10	100
Bent-over Rowing 52	1	10	50	2	10	75	3	10	100
Bench Press 53	1	10	60	2	10	90	3	10	120
Upright Rowing 54	1	10	40	2	10	60	3	10	80
Dumbbell Pullover 56	1	10	35	2	10	45	3	10	55
Barbell Curl 57	1	10	50	2	10	60	3	10	70
Two-hand Dumbbell									
Extension 58	1	10	35	2	10	40	3	10	45
Reverse Curl 59	1	10	40	2	10	50	3	10	60
Front Squat 60	1	10	60	2	10	90	3	10	120
Donkey Calf Raise 62	1	15		2	20		3	25	
Leg Raise 47	1	15		2	20		3	25	
Seated Twist 63	1	25		2	25		3	25	
Relaxation									

PRESS BEHIND NECK

Purpose: This is a very good exercise for developing width in the shoulders and a squared-off look to the deltoids. If you lower the bar all the way down until it rests on the shoulders you'll work trapezius as well as deltoids. If you stop when bar is touching neck you'll work mainly frontal and lateral deltoids.

Equipment: Barbell

Procedure: 1. Take barbell resting on shoulders behind neck, inhale, and press overhead until arms are almost locked out. 2. Lower slowly to starting position. Exhale.

BENT-OVER ROWING

Purpose: This exercise is the best all-around back developer. Depending on how you do this movement, you'll get different results. If you keep the upper body stationary and pull the bar up to the chest you'll work the central latissimus dorsi area. If you raise the upper body upward as you pull the bar up to touch just below the rib cage you'll work the spinal erectors and trapezius and the lats too but not as directly as in the first position.

Equipment: Barbell

Procedure: Stand on the floor or on a bench, bend forward at waist until upper body is parallel with floor, keeping knees slightly bent. 2. Grip barbell with slightly wider than shoulder-width grip and inhale. 3. Pull barbell up until it touches chest. 4. Exhale as you slowly lower bar to starting position. Be sure to get a good stretch as you lower the bar.

BENCH PRESS

Purpose: Bench press is probably the most popular upper body exercise. It is done lying down. When you do bench presses for any length of time, progress is usually fast. The movement is primarily for developing the pectoral muscles, but the frontal deltoids and triceps muscles receive some work as well.

Equipment: Flat bench and barbell

Procedure: 1. Lie on bench, feet resting on floor, and grasp a barbell with a slightly wider than shoulder-width grip. 2. Inhale and lower barbell slowly to chest, touching chest at the bottom portion of the pectorals. 3. As soon as bar touches chest, press it upward until arms almost lock out. Exhale.

UPRIGHT ROWING

Purpose: This is one of the most effective exercises to develop the trapezius and frontal deltoid muscles.

Equipment: Barbell (or two dumbbells if preferred)

Procedure: 1. Hold barbell in front of thighs at a distance of about six to 12 inches and inhale. 2. Pull barbell up until it gently touches chin. 3. Exhale as you allow barbell slowly to return to starting position.

DUMBBELL PULLOVER

Purpose: This exercise works the rib cage, the serratus (the jagged, sawtooth muscles between the lats and the pectorals) and the rear head of the triceps. Lie crossways on a flat bench to provide more stretch.

Equipment: Flat bench and a dumbbell

Procedure: 1. Lie across a flat bench and hold a dumbbell between hands directly overhead. 2. Inhale and lower dumbbell in an arc so that it moves behind head and almost touches floor. 3. Raise the dumbbell, feeling the tension in the serratus, rib cage and triceps. Stop when the dumbbell is directly overhead. Exhale.

BARBELL CURL

Purpose: This is the basic exercise for building the biceps. It should be done slowly, especially as the weight is lowered, and without much back bending.

Equipment: Barbell

Procedure: 1. Stand holding a barbell, hands approximately shoulder width, and palms facing away from body. 2. Inhale, and holding elbows stationary at sides, curl the barbell up in an arc until it barely touches the chin. 3. Exhale as you slowly lower the weight to starting position.

TWO-HAND DUMBBELL EXTENSION

Purpose: If the elbows are held so that they are pointing outward when doing this exercise, it will work the outer triceps. If the elbows point straight ahead, the rear head of the triceps will be worked. If the elbows are held midway between straight ahead and sideways, all heads of the triceps will be worked.

Equipment: A dumbbell

Procedure: 1. Stand and grasp the dumbbell between both hands in an overhead position. 2. Inhale and lower dumbbell slowly as low as possible (lean slightly backward so that the weight can descend to its lowest). 3. Return the dumbbell to starting position, using the triceps muscles until the dumbbell is overhead and the elbows are slightly unlocked. Exhale.

REVERSE CURL

Purpose: One of the best movements to develop the top part of the forearms and strengthen the grip. Be sure to squeeze the bar hard when curling.

Equipment: Barbell

Procedure: 1. Stand holding barbell with palms facing toward body. 2. Inhale and curl barbell upward in an arc until barbell touches chin. 3. Exhale as you slowly lower barbell to starting position.

FRONT SQUAT

Purpose: Front squats (bar held in front) are often used as an alternative to regular squats. Not as much weight is used since the barbell is held in front of the shoulders. The movement, however, works the thighs more directly than regular squat (which works the hips somewhat). Front squats work the entire thigh, especially the frontal portion. As in regular squat, do not lock knees at the completion of each rep.

Equipment: Barbell and 2″ x 4″ block

Procedure: 1. Assume starting position with heels on block and feet approximately 12 inches apart. Hold barbell on shoulders. 2. Looking straight ahead and keeping back straight, inhale and descend until bottoms of thighs are parallel with the floor. 3. Start ascending and stop when you reach starting position. Exhale.

Some Useful Information about Calf Work

The calf muscles are developed by rising up and going down on the toes. All exercises that develop the calves are called "calf raises." The position of the toes (whether toes are pointing straight ahead, inward, or outward), whether the knees are straight or bent, and where the center of gravity is located in the foot as the heel is raised, all determine how the calf muscles will develop. Calf raises of any variety done with toes out and rising so that the center of gravity in the foot is on the ball of the foot and the big toe will work the inner head of the calf. Calf raises done with toes pointing in and rising so that the center of gravity in the foot is on the outer portion of the foot and the little toe will work the outer head of the calf. Raises done with the heel rising straight upward will develop both heads of the calf. It is very important to get a full range of movement in this exercise by going as far up and down on the toes as is possible. For this reason a calf block is used.

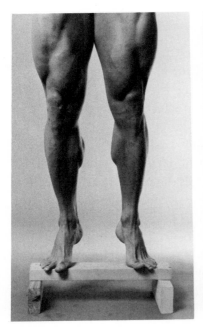
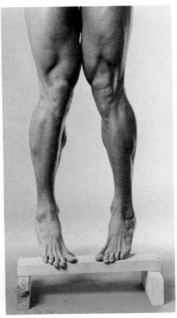
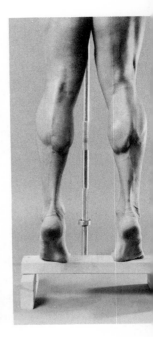

DONKEY CALF RAISE

Purpose: "Donkeys" are a great way to build good overall calf development. When done correctly they form the foundation of calf training. They can be done with toes pointing in, out, or straight ahead, and with knees locked or bent, for different effects on the development of the calf muscles.

Equipment: A person to sit on the small of the lower back, right above the hips. Select someone whose body weight is about equal to yours. However, if your partner is lighter, have him or her hold a barbell plate. You'll also need a calf block and something to hold on to.

Procedure: 1. Position feet on calf block. 2. Bend forward at waist and hold onto a bench for support. 3. Have partner get on your back (he or she can step up from a low stool if necessary). 4. Inhale and rise as high as possible on toes. 5. Exhale as you descend, heels downward as low as they can go.

SEATED TWIST

Purpose: This exercise works the sides—the intercostals and external oblique abdominals. It also helps tighten up the lower back and trim any "spare tire" one may have acquired.

Equipment: Four- to five-foot pole; a bench, or a chair with a low back

Procedure: Sit on bench with legs straddling each side and pole resting on shoulders behind neck. 2. Inhale and twist to the right. 3. Exhale as you twist left (steps 2 and 3 are one repetition), keeping the stomach muscles tensed as you twist to each side.

5 · The Basic Split Routine: Program III

In this program the split routine is introduced. Exercises for deltoids, chest and triceps (the pushing muscles) are done one day and exercises for the back, biceps, forearms (pulling muscles) and thighs and calves are done on the next day. Abdominals are worked every training day. Thus the whole body is exercised completely in two-day cycles. This program can be used by a man of any age provided he has progressed through the previous basic programs or if he has been already training for some time and is in good enough shape to do the four-day-per-week program. This routine is followed four days a week for the beginning and intermediate stages and five days a week for the advanced stage. For example, beginners and intermediates work back, biceps, forearms, legs and abs on Monday and Thursday and shoulders, chest, triceps and abs on Tuesday and Friday. Advanced trainees work out five days a week and take weekends off. Monday, Wednesday, Friday: back, biceps, forearms, legs, abs are worked; on Tuesday and Thursday, shoulders, chest, triceps and abs are worked. The following week the days are reversed: On Monday, Wednesday, and Friday

shoulders, chest, and triceps and abs are worked, while on Tuesday and Thursday, back, biceps, forearms, legs and abs are trained.

Notice that opposing groups of muscles are trained on alternate days. This way the body parts that have been exercised on the previous day get a rest and are able to recuperate and grow.

Train at the beginner's level for at least two weeks before you progress to the intermediate level. You should experience very slight soreness the day following a workout. This is normal and means your body is responding. If the soreness is intense, it means you are doing too much and you should cut back on the sets. You can train at the intermediate level for as long as you feel you are making gains. When this program gets too easy and you feel you're ready for five-day-a-week training, move on to the advanced level.

PROGRAM III BASIC SPLIT ROUTINE

MONDAY AND THURSDAY

	page	BEGINNER			INTERMEDIATE			ADVANCED		
		sets	reps	weight	sets	reps	weight	sets	reps	weight
Mental Preparation										
BACK										
Wide Grip Chins	68–69	2	8	0	3	10	0	4	12	0
Bent-over Rowing	52	2	10	100	3	10	120	4	10	140
Dumbbell Rowing	70	2	10	40	3	10	50	4	10	60
BICEPS										
Barbell Curl	57	2	8	70	3	8	85	4	8	100
Alternate Dumbbell Curl	71	2	8	30	3	8	40	4	8	50
Dumbbell Concentration Curl	72	2	10	25	3	10	30	4	10	35
FOREARMS										
Reverse Curl	59	2	10	60	3	10	70	4	10	80
THIGHS										
Squat	72–73	2	10	135	3	10	155	4	10	175
Hack Squat	74	2	10	20	3	10	25	4	10	30
Leg Lunge	75	2	10	20	3	10	30	4	10	40
CALF										
Donkey Calf Raise	62	3	15	*	4	20	*	5	25	*
One-legged Calf Raise	76	2	15	0	3	15	0	4	15	0
ABDOMINALS										
Sit-up Over Bench	77	2	15	0	3	20	0	4	25	0
Incline Knee-in	78	2	15	0	3	20	0	4	25	0
Seated Twist	63	2	15	0	3	20	0	4	25	0
Relaxation										

* Partner your weight.

PROGRAM III BASIC SPLIT ROUTINE

(CONTINUED)

TUESDAY AND FRIDAY

	page	BEGINNER			INTERMEDIATE			ADVANCED		
		sets	reps	weight	sets	reps	weight	sets	reps	weight
Mental Preparation										
SHOULDERS										
Dumbbell Press	79	2	10	40	3	10	50	4	10	60
Dumbbell Shrug	80	2	10	40	3	10	50	4	10	60
Dumbbell Lateral Raise	81	2	10	15	3	10	20	4	10	25
Dumbbell Rear Raise	82	2	10	15	3	10	20	4	10	25
CHEST										
Bench Press	53	2	10	120	3	10	150	4	10	180
Incline Press	83	2	10	100	3	10	125	4	10	150
Dumbbell Flys	84	2	10	25	3	10	30	4	10	35
Dumbbell Pullover	56	2	10	50	3	10	55	4	10	60
TRICEPS										
Close Grip Bench Press	85	2	10	70	3	10	85	4	10	100
Lying Triceps Extension	86	2	10	50	3	10	65	4	10	80
One-arm Dumbbell Extension	87	2	8	20	3	8	25	4	8	30
ABDOMINALS										
Sit-up Over Bench	77	2	15	0	3	20	0	4	25	0
Incline Knee-in	78	2	15	0	3	20	0	4	25	0
Seated Twist	63	2	15	0	3	20	0	4	25	0
Relaxation										

Advanced trainees do the same workout as intermediates but train 5 times a week as explained previously and do 4 sets of each exercise.

WIDE GRIP CHINS

Purpose: Wide grip chins is one of the very best ways to build a wide, V-shaped upper back. It can be done by pulling up until chin touches bar (front chins) or until bar touches behind neck. (Chins behind neck work the trapezius and some of the smaller muscles of the upper back more directly, while front chins work more serratus.)

Equipment: Overhead bar

Procedure: 1. Grasp overhead bar with wide grip (slightly wider than shoulder width). 2. Inhale, and pull yourself up until chin either touches bar (as in front chin) or until bar touches behind neck (chin behind neck). 3. Exhale as you slowly lower yourself to starting position.

DUMBBELL ROWING

Purpose: To build the outer section of the lats and accentuate the taper of the back. It is important to hold onto a bench or other stationary object so that the upper body can be kept stationary.

Equipment: One dumbbell and a bench for support

Procedure: 1. Spread feet about two feet apart and bend knees slightly. Bend forward at waist and support upper body with one hand, keeping the upper body parallel to the floor. 2. With free hand grasp a dumbbell, inhale and pull upward until it touches chest. 3. Lower dumbbell to the floor as you exhale. Be sure to lower the dumbbell as far as possible to work the lower lats. 4. Repeat movement with other arm after resting about 20 seconds.

ALTERNATE DUMBBELL CURL

Purpose: This is my favorite biceps exercise. It works the biceps fully because the wrist can be turned outward as the dumbbell is curled upward. This is not possible with a barbell. It is important to establish a rhythm as this movement is done.

Equipment: Two dumbbells

Procedure: 1. Stand holding a dumbbell in each hand. 2. Inhale and curl one of the dumbbells upward. As you curl, turn your wrist outward. 3. Stop when dumbbell touches shoulder. 4. Exhale as you lower dumbbell to starting position. 5. Repeat with other arm. This constitutes one repetition.

DUMBBELL CONCENTRATION CURL

Purpose: This is the best exercise for developing a peak to the biceps. It is very important to keep the wrist straight, as in all curling movements, and not to let the elbow come in too close to the body when doing this exercise.

Equipment: One dumbbell

Procedure: 1. Bend forward at waist, put one hand on knee and with other hand grasp a dumbbell. Let it hang so that it almost touches the floor. 2. Inhale and curl dumbbell until the arm is bent as much as possible and the biceps is fully contracted. 3. Slowly lower the weight to starting position. Exhale.

SQUAT

Purpose: To add size to the thigh muscles. Squats are great for gaining weight and for increasing endurance when done in high reps. Squats work all the major muscles of the thighs when performed correctly. Be sure to keep the back straight and do the movement slowly. Do not lock the knees completely at the completion of each rep, as locking the knees takes tension off the thigh muscles, and tension should be maintained. Don't squat down past a position where the bottoms of the thighs are parallel with the floor. Squatting slowly into parallel position works the leg biceps. Focus on a spot straight in front of you and if possible look into a mirror while squatting (this will help you check your position and form). Use padding around the barbell to protect your neck and upper back if needed (barbell should rest on upper back and not on the neck). Do not bounce at the bottom of the movement. It is possible to injure the knees and/or lower back if you are careless doing squats. They are a great exercise for stimulating muscular growth throughout the whole body.

Equipment: Barbell, a 2" x 4" block to place under your heels for better balance and a way to get the barbell behind your neck. It can be handed to you or you can lift it up yourself and place it on your shoulders. If the weight is too heavy to do this, you should use squat racks.

Procedure: 1. Assume starting position with heels on block and feet about 12 to 18 inches apart, barbell resting on shoulders (top of upper back) behind neck. 2. Inhale and descend into squat until bottoms of thighs are parallel with floor. 3. Start upward and continue until you return to starting position. Exhale.

HACK SQUAT

Purpose: For building the frontal thigh muscles, especially those above the knees, this movement is unexcelled. I always get a fantastic pump in the thighs when I do hacks following regular squats in my routine. Keep knees unlocked at completion of each rep as shown in photo.

Equipment: 2" x 4" block to place under heels for balance, a pair of dumbbells (as shown) or a barbell (or hack squat machine if you have access to one)

Procedure: 1. Stand with heels on block and feet 12 to 18 inches apart, holding dumbbells at sides. Inhale. 2. Descend to position where bottoms of thighs are parallel to floor. 3. Start ascending until you reach starting position, standing with knees slightly bent. Exhale.

LEG LUNGE*

Purpose: Lunges work the entire thigh but are especially effective for delineating the inner and outer thigh. Care should be taken not to take too-big steps at first or descending into the lunge too low, which might put a strain in the groin area.

Equipment: Light barbell (as shown) or 2 dumbbells

Procedure: 1. With a light barbell resting on shoulders, feet about one foot apart, inhale. 2. Take a step forward about three to four feet and dip down into lunge position until knee of back leg almost touches floor. 3. Return to starting position, exhale, and repeat with other leg.

* This exercise is also very effective using no weights and higher repetitions. Anyone including lunges in his program should start without weights.

ONE-LEGGED CALF RAISE

Purpose: This exercise primarily works the gastrocnemius muscle, both inner and outer heads. It is a great way to pace your calf workout by doing sets for each leg without stopping until the whole routine is completed. And what a pump!

Equipment: The exercise can be done on a calf block while holding a stationary object or a person for support, or on one of the steps of a stairway. When you get stronger, a dumbbell can be held in one hand for added resistance.

Procedure: 1. Position foot on calf block. 2. As you steady yourself for support, inhale and rise as high as possible on the toes. 3. Pause for an instant. 4. Descend on heel as low as possible as you exhale. After doing selected amount of reps with one leg, repeat procedure for the other.

SIT-UP OVER BENCH (ROMAN CHAIR SIT-UP)

Purpose: This exercise works the upper part of the rectus abdominals. If done with a twist to each side it will work the external oblique abdominals and intercostals.

Equipment: Flat bench and a means to anchor feet to floor

Procedure: 1. Sit sideways on a flat bench and anchor feet to floor. (Either place them under a barbell or a stationary object or have someone hold them.) 2. Inhale and lower upper body until it is almost parallel with floor. 3. Exhale as you return to starting position. Keep the abdominals tensed throughout all repetitions.

INCLINE KNEE-IN

Purpose: This is a good movement for the lower rectus abdominals. It is easier to do than leg raises (which also work lower abs). The difficulty of the exercise can be increased by increasing the angle of the bench.

Equipment: Bench and block to raise one end of bench

Procedure: 1. Lie flat on bench with hands under hips and legs straight out. 2. Inhale and bring knees in until they touch chest. 3. Exhale as you straighten legs out slowly to starting position.

DUMBBELL PRESS

Purpose: At least one pressing movement should be done to exercise the deltoids, and dumbbell press is one of the best. Each deltoid must work separately to raise the dumbbells. The weights should be pressed straight overhead. If you lean back, you put more tension on the front deltoids. This exercise can be done seated or standing.

Equipment: Two dumbbells and flat bench (the last is optional)

Procedure: 1. Hold dumbbells at shoulders, inhale, and press weights straight overhead until the arms are almost locked out. 2. Lower dumbbells slowly until they again touch shoulders. Exhale.

DUMBBELL SHRUG

Purpose: This exercise works the trapezius very directly. It also affects the muscles of the neck somewhat.

Equipment: Two dumbbells

Procedure: 1. Hold a dumbbell in each hand at each side. 2. As you inhale, pull up your shoulders toward your ears as far as they will go. 3. Let shoulders slowly drop to starting position as you exhale.

DUMBBELL LATERAL RAISE (SIDE RAISE)

Purpose: This exercise works the lateral deltoids very directly. Be sure to turn the wrist outward as the dumbbells are raised to the sides: this places more tension on the lateral and rear deltoid. Keep the arms slightly unlocked at the elbows when doing the movement.

Equipment: Two dumbbells

Procedure: 1. Start with hands at sides holding each dumbbell. 2. Inhale, and raise the dumbbells, turning wrists outward and keeping the elbows slightly unlocked. 3. When arms reach a position where they are parallel to the floor, lower the dumbbells slowly to starting position. Exhale.

DUMBBELL REAR RAISE

Purpose: This is an excellent way to develop the rear deltoid. The dumbbells should be raised to the sides but they should be brought slightly forward also. Be sure to turn wrists outward as dumbbells are raised.

Equipment: Two dumbbells and a bench

Procedure: 1. Sit on the edge of a bench, bend forward at the waist and grasp a dumbbell in each hand. 2. Inhale and raise the dumbbells sideways but slightly forward, turning the wrist outward as you do so. 3. When you cannot raise the weights any higher, slowly allow them to descend to starting position. Exhale.

INCLINE PRESS

Purpose: This is the best exercise for developing the upper pectorals (pectoralis minor). I find an incline of 45 degrees to be best for working this area.

Equipment: Incline bench and barbell

Procedure: Lie on incline bench and grasp a barbell overhead with a slightly wider than shoulder width grip. Inhale. 2. Lower barbell slowly until it touches upper pectoral muscles. 3. Press barbell upward until arms are almost locked out. Exhale.

DUMBBELL FLYS

Purpose: For developing the outer part of the pectorals, this is my favorite exercise. Be sure to lower weights as far down as possible in order to work this section fully.

Equipment: Flat bench and two dumbbells

Procedure: 1. Lie on back on flat bench, grasping a dumbbell in each hand over chest. 2. Inhale and lower dumbbells to sides with elbows slightly unlocked—go as low as possible. 3. Raise dumbbells in an arc to starting position. Exhale. Always keep the arms unlocked at the same angle throughout the movement.

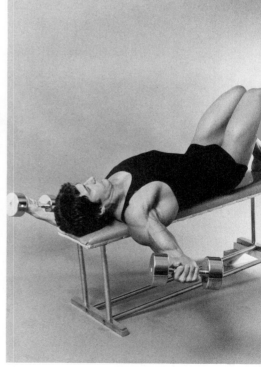

CLOSE GRIP BENCH PRESS

Purpose: This exercise is very good for developing the outer head of the triceps, but only if it is done with the elbows pointing straight out to the sides. The weight must travel straight up to get a maximum pump in the outer triceps.

Equipment: Barbell and a flat bench

Procedure: 1. Lie on back on flat bench and grasp a barbell with hands 6 to 12 inches apart. 2. Inhale and slowly lower barbell to bottom of pectorals. Touch pectorals with bar and push bar up until elbows are almost locked out. Exhale.

LYING TRICEPS EXTENSION

Purpose: One of the best movements for building size of the rear head of the triceps. The elbows should be kept about one foot apart and the upper arms should stay parallel throughout the movement.

Equipment: Flat bench and a barbell

Procedure: 1. Lie on bench and grasp barbell, hands about 12 inches apart. 2. Inhale slowly and lower the barbell to a position behind the head. 3. Raise the barbell until it is directly over your eyes. Exhale.

ONE-ARM DUMBBELL EXTENSION

Purpose: One-arm dumbbell extension is a triceps exercise that works the rear head of the triceps especially well. It's important to first warm up the elbows by using a light weight on your first set and to lower the dumbbell as far as possible behind shoulders with each rep.

Equipment: One dumbbell

Procedure: 1. With one hand on your hip for support, hold the dumbbell straight overhead with the other hand; inhale. 2. Slowly lower dumbbell behind shoulder, keeping upper arm parallel to head and neck. Lower dumbbell as far as possible. 3. Exhale as you extend dumbbell to finish position (in finish position elbow should be bent very slightly). 4. Change hands after each set is completed.

PART III

Bodybuilding
for Women

6 · A Beautiful Body

WHY EXERCISE?

Having good muscle tone and being physically fit do not have to be synonymous with big muscles. The exercises that follow are designed for women of all ages and at all levels of physical fitness. They will help you get fit and stay fit, help you be full of energy and look slimmer while staying supple. If you need to gain weight or inches, you will find the routines easily adapted to your needs also.

Even though you know all the healthful benefits of exercise, it can be difficult at first to stick to your program. There are literally hundreds of books written on how to shape up, how to exercise and how to diet. Many of them will give you varying degrees of success, depending on how faithfully you are doing them. But that can be a problem for many people—being able to be faithful in following a routine of diet and exercise. You need motivation, and this may be hard to find, much less to sustain. This is a difficult problem to solve for someone else—yet I can relate to you how I motivate myself to stick to my routine, and at the same time I may possibly give you some helpful suggestions. Remember, however, that motivation cannot be something made up or make-believe; it must be very real to you. When I first met Frank I was already conscious of my body and had been taking pretty good care of myself by exercising moderately and watching my diet; but I was basically a heavy person, and unless I watched myself very carefully I could gain ten unnecessary pounds within a week. And being in a family where three large meals were prepared daily, and loving to eat, it was difficult for me to keep my weight down. When I began spending most of my time with Frank it became easier. It seemed that being around someone else who was into staying in shape and staying healthy really made it easier for me to do the same. Even though Frank was more concerned with keeping his weight up, and I wanted to hold mine down, just being around someone who was always in superior physical condition gave me the motivation I needed to stick to my program. I don't think others should be expected to follow my advice, or my husband's, or to believe that what we say works, unless we ourselves follow that advice. Frank's being in the public eye year round (and my traveling with him as his photographer) is one motivation I always have.

Another motivation I have *always* had is that when I look good, I feel good. In fact, I feel *terrific!* It is such a fantastic feeling that it is worth 200 times whatever sacrifices I had to make to look like that and stay like that. My energy level is so high that it is unexplainable. It has to be felt. I also choose clothes that fit me *only* when I'm in shape. I will never purchase an article of clothing larger than my "in shape" size. That way, if I want to look good, I can't just hide in a larger size. I must get in shape and stay in shape to look good.

Motivations are personal. I can't tell you to get in shape and stay there because you want to please someone else or to fit into a new outfit. These may not matter too much to you. You must find something you care about deeply and let this motivate you. Some people are able to motivate themselves by means of rewards every now and then. If you are one of them, reward yourself when you feel you have overcome an obstacle or have met a goal connected with your idea of how you want to look or feel. I believe it is important to reward yourself as you go along. Ask your friends to say something if they notice that you are making progress. This will give you a constant verbal reward. Also, ask them not to say anything negative if your progress does not show immediately. Have them keep their comments neutral in that case. If you are constantly hearing how great you look it is easier to stay headed toward your goal. If someone should make some unkind remarks (even if they are true), use them as an incentive to work at your goal even much harder. Don't let anyone or anything get you down. It will be more than worth it, once you reach your goal.

The "reward" method is very good as long as you are not harming yourself or working against yourself with the types of rewards you give yourself. Stay away from rewards such as a week off from exercising or indulging in a "forbidden food" that will wreck your program. Instead, reward yourself with a beauty treatment at a spa or facial salon. Buy yourself a new article of clothing. Pamper yourself in some way. Do things that make for improvement, not destruction. If you really want to reward yourself with food, do it healthfully. Don't "junk it up"; it will be much easier to stay on a healthful path afterward if you do it with healthful meals. Go out for a meal. Splurge at a restaurant you've always wanted to go to. Eat a good balanced meal. Choose foods you wouldn't normally cook at home because of the trouble or difficulty in preparing them. Have something you really consider a treat—Beef Wellington, for example. Another way to reward yourself is to give yourself the gift of time. Give yourself a day off. Don't stick to your regular routine. Go out for a brisk walk, ride a bicycle, go skating, play! Spend some time relaxing and being with yourself as well as with good friends. Pamper yourself. If you live with others, let them know that this is your day and you're going to spend it as you wish. Ask them not to request unnecessary jobs or favors from you on this day. This should be *your* day, spent entirely as you choose.

GETTING READY

I have selected exercises which I have found to work wonders for both figure and stamina. Some of the exercises may appear tough at first. You can't expect to master new movements immediately. You need to begin slowly, familiarizing yourself with each exercise. It is like learning to play an instrument—even if you're a natural, it takes a little practice. I believe you will find the training routines easy and comfortable to follow and very effective for your needs. These routines are basically directed to women between the approximate ages of eighteen and fifty, at all levels of experience with training.

You will find listed two styles of training, one using no special equipment, and one incorporating the use of weight-training apparatus. Both are designed to give you optimum results. Free-form exercises with no equipment tend to give you added suppleness, and a long, more shapely and slimmer appearance. Your daily activities may give you a clue as to what part of your body you wish to put emphasis on. If you sit a lot during the day you should put your exercise emphasis on your hips and thighs. Athletic women may wish to train for better control in their particular sport. Sports provide good exercise but usually work only an isolated part of the body. Sports in combination with free exercise or weight training seem to be more effective than sports alone as a method of shaping up.

Let's prepare ourselves for a workout. You will need some comfortable clothes to wear. Do not wear street clothes to exercise in. They are not made for this purpose. They are often tight and binding, with lumpy zippers and buttons that could cause discomfort in many of the postures you will be taking in your exercises. Instead, choose light clothing, without buttons, zippers and hooks, in which your body will be able to move freely. Leotards and tights are ideal because they give you freedom while fitting snugly, thus helping you avoid getting caught on the equipment or tangling during your movements. Leotards and tights also give you a clear view of your body, so you are able to constantly check your figure for progress. Sweatsuits, workout shorts, etc., are also good. The main concern is to be comfortable and free from restrictions. I suggest, when you are training on a carpeted surface, that you wear leotards and a soft foot covering or go barefoot. If you train on a hard surface, a good pair of shoes that support your feet would serve you best.

Now you are ready to choose a space to exercise in. You will need a space where you will have plenty of room to do the movements. It is also helpful if you can view yourself in a mirror when you train. This will enable you to monitor your movements. You should feel comfortable with the space you choose. It should be free of distractions, noise and interruptions. You should be able to concentrate and relax in the area. Try to perform your routine in the same space each time you train.

The time period in which you choose to exercise is just as important as the space. I find my energy level at its highest approximately three hours after my morning meal, and two hours after my midday meal. I usually train at either of these times because my body is awake, the circulation has increased, and I have been properly nourished. Whatever you decide is best for you, be sure to allow at least two hours between the time you eat and the time you exercise. If you are only having a snack, allow 45 minutes to an hour. You want to give your food time to digest and supply you with energy. Eating and exercising together can cause an upset stomach, poor digestion and a poorly done routine.

CONCENTRATION

Since you will be training regularly, you will most likely be forming new habits—habits which will also carry over into your usual daily activities. Concentrate and stay aware of how you look when you move. Keep your movements graceful during your exercises as well as during the periods between your exercises. Watch how you hold your entire body. Look at yourself as though you were viewing someone else. In staying aware of your movements and appearance during the exercises, you will notice yourself developing flattering habits which will follow through in everything you do. Fluid, graceful movements will come naturally. The key to accomplishing this successfully is relaxation. Turn your thoughts away from the outside distractions and tune inward to your body. Relax your body but stay mentally alert and in total control of all your movements. Always be aware of your total body even when your concentration is on the exercise or a specific muscle group. Your total concentration can also work to help you shape up in a shorter period of time and cause your workouts to be more effective. You should always get the maximum benefit from every movement. During each exercise concentrate on the movement *and* the muscle group being worked. Cause the muscle to be worked by the mental as well as the physical force. Concentrating on specific muscles helps direct the blood more quickly to these areas, causing increased circulation and added energy, as well as helping to repair the muscles.

GOAL SETTING

I have always kept a journal. In the journal I put anything that seems important to me and my progress. No matter how unrelated the subject of my journal might be, it all relates in the end to what I am or what I've become. I have found that by using this journal to spell out my goals in detail I work toward them with seemingly little effort. Also very effective in reaching goals associated with your body is to draw a picture of yourself looking the way you would like to look. If you're too thin, have a picture of yourself a little heavier, yet shapely. If you are too heavy, draw a picture of yourself a bit thinner. Be realistic in these goals. (If you're short don't imagine yourself as tall—such a goal would be unrealistic.) It doesn't matter how good the drawing is—it is your image and in your private journal. As long as you can visualize it, that's all that is necessary. Study this picture at least three times a day, every day. (Before each meal and training session are good times to do this.) If you wish to change your goals or your picture of yourself, do so. The main concern is to get it down in writing, and in detail. During your Mental Preparation (done before every exercise session) you will be visualizing these images of yourself and your goals. Study them carefully. Know what you want to do with yourself.

Once your goals are realized, set new goals. Constantly improve yourself. Take before and after photos and compare them. Often you may get discouraged and feel you are not progressing. You probably have forgotten exactly where you came from and where you're at now in comparison. The pictures will help remind you and give you the incentive to continue.

THE ROUTINES

In Chapters 7 and 8 you will find two divisions: Exercising Free Form and Exercising with Weights. In each of these you will find three excellent exercise routines to ease you into your new program and help you realize your goals. You will notice that all three of the routines—Basic, Middle and Success—are divided into three levels of progression: Beginner, Intermediate and Advanced. Start each routine at the Beginner's level. Do the movements and low repetitions for a few days. If you are a Beginner allow *at least* one week per level before progressing. When you reach the Advanced level, remain there until the exercises have become too easy and you no longer feel that they are benefiting your body. Then it is time to move to the Middle Routine, following the same progression. Last, move to the Success Routine. Once you have reached the Success Routine on the Advanced level and you are no longer receiving benefits—this could take several weeks or even several months—the next step is to further personalize your program. On the exercises that work an area you would like to reduce more, you should gradually increase the number of sets and repetitions you do. If your concern is to gain inches in some areas, you should keep the sets and repetitions fewer or the same (depending on what you can handle), but do them very slowly and concentratedly. Add more poundage. On free-form leg exercises you may wish to use ankle weights to help concentrate the effects.

If you have been exercising regularly, you will want to move through the Basic Routine quickly (one week), into the Middle Routine for approximately two to three weeks, and then stay with each level of the Success Routine until you feel you should advance. Once you have reached a point where you are constantly getting benefit from your routine, stick with that routine. With this regularly repeated routine your progress will continue to increase with each workout. All the exercises should be slightly difficult after the first half of the repetitions.

Each routine (Basic, Middle, or Success) of exercising free form or exercising with weights is to be practiced three times each week on alternate days, i.e., Monday, Wednesday and Friday, or Tuesday, Thursday and Saturday.

7 · Exercising Free Form

BASIC ROUTINE

The first series of exercises has been designed to meet the needs of those women who consider themselves beginners. If you have never followed an exercise program regularly (at least three days per week), if you have not been exercising a great deal recently, or if you have been doing a slow-paced exercise program, you should use this routine as a starting point. This routine requires no special equipment. It emphasizes keeping supple and youthful in your movements, limbering and preparing your body for an effective start toward your goal. It is essential that everyone begin with this program. Each person may then progress at her own speed.

BASIC ROUTINE

EXERCISE/PAGE	BE-GINNER		INTER-MEDIATE		AD-VANCED		Purpose
	sets	reps	sets	reps	sets	reps	
Mental Preparation							
Jumping Jacks 106	1	10	1	15	1	25	Warm-up
Straddle Swing 105	1	8	1	10	1	20	"
Body Stretch 106	1	8	1	10	1	20	"
Track Start 104	1	15	1	25	1	30	"
Twist and Kick 115	1	15	1	20	1	25	Waist
Trim Sits 116	1	8	1	10	1	15	"
Stomach Firmer 113	1	8	1	10	1	15	Abdomen
Alternate Upright Knee-in 108	1	10	1	15	1	20	"
Heel Clicks 121	1	10	1	20	1	25	Buttocks
Kneeling Knee to Chest 119	1	10	1	20	1	25	Hips & Butt.
Leg Overs 125	1	10	1	15	1	20	"
Inner Thigh Stretch 126	1	10	1	20	1	30	Inner Thigh
Modified Push-ups 134	1	8	1	15	1	20	Chest
Swan Lift 129	1	5	1	10	1	15	Back
Arm Circles 130	1	15	1	20	1	25	Arms
Shoulder Shrug and Circle 128	1	10	1	15	1	20	Shoulder
Relaxation							

MIDDLE ROUTINE

This next routine has been designed specifically for women who presently exercise a moderate amount (two times per week). The general areas which give women the most trouble seem to be the hips and waistline. Unless we exercise, it seems that when we reach adulthood we find extra weight being put on our outer thighs, and our hips become wider. The waistline also tends to widen with age. This routine gives your whole body a vigorous workout with a good general fitness routine, as well as putting extra emphasis on these important trouble areas. No equipment is needed to do this routine. You will notice the routine begins with three warm-up exercises and then moves directly into waistline and abdomen exercises. You are exercising your waistline first, while your energy level is at its highest. Be sure your stomach is *close* to empty (not starved) when you begin; this will insure a comfortable and effective workout for this body area.

MIDDLE ROUTINE

EXERCISE/PAGE	BE-GINNER sets	reps	INTER-MEDIATE sets	reps	AD-VANCED sets	reps	Purpose
Mental Preparation							
Good Morning 101	1	10	1	12	1	15	Warm-up
Spinal Stretch 103	1	6	1	8	1	10	"
Track Start 104	1	5	1	10	1	15	"
Alternate Upright Knee-in 108	1	10	1	15	1	20	Waist, Abdomen
Leg Spread Tummy Trimmer 109	1	8	1	12	1	20	"
Leg Raise & Circle 110	1	8	1	12	1	20	"
Alternate Elbow-to-knee Twist 111	1	8	1	12	1	20	"
Bent-over Twist 112	1	15	2	15	2	30	"
Alternate Thigh Stretch 117	1	8	1	15	1	25	Hip, Thigh
Kneeling Side Leg Lift 118	1	10	1	15	1	20	"
Kneeling Knee to Chest 119	1	15	2	15	2	30	"
Leg Spread & Cross 120	1	15	1	20	1	25	"
Heel Clicks 121	1	6	2	15	1	30	Buttock
Three-position Calf Raise 122	1	10	1	15	1	25	Calf
Neck Rolls 127	1	8	1	10	1	15	Neck
Modified Push-ups 134	1	8	1	10	1	15	Chest
Side Lateral Raise 131	1	6	1	10	1	15	Deltoid
Shoulder Shrug & Circle 128	1	5	1	10	1	12	Shoulder
Relaxation							

SUCCESS ROUTINE

I call this the Success Routine because here you are working out at your maximum. You should be very familiar with the movements before advancing. *Before* you begin this routine you should already have been following a regular exercise program of some kind for at least the past six months (something along the lines of the Middle Routine is perfect).

The following routine has been designed specifically for women who are experienced in their exercising and aware of the movements they need to reach their goal. These exercises will give you all-over body conditioning, with equal attention paid to all body parts, and will help you to maintain a reasonable amount of flexibility and suppleness. Many new exercises have been added to those already found in the previous routines. The sets and repetitions have been altered to fit the advanced student. No equipment is needed to do this routine. Since all women tend to need more work on the hip area, there will be a slight emphasis on this area, and of course, overall body flexibility. After you have done your three warm-up exercises— which are also excellent for the hips and thighs—you will begin a series of leg and hip exercises which are highly concentrated on working this area. I suggest that they be done at a moderate-to-fast pace, after you have begun slowly and familiarized yourself with the movement.

SUCCESS ROUTINE

EXERCISE/PAGE	BE-GINNER sets	reps	INTER-MEDIATE sets	reps	AD-VANCED sets	reps	Purpose
Mental Preparation							
Track Start 104	1	15	1	15	1	20	Warm-up
Straddle Swing 105	1	8	1	10	1	15	"
Jumping Jacks 106	1	10	1	20	1	25	"
Rear Leg Lift 123	1	8	1	12	2	25	Hips/ Buttocks
Heel Clicks 121	1	8	1	12	2	30	"
Kneeling Knee to Chest 119	1	15	2	10	2	30	"
Kneeling Side Leg Lift 118	1	10	1	15	2	25	"
Side Leg Circles 124	1	10	1	15	1	40	"
Leg Spread and Cross 120	1	15	1	20	2	30	Outer & Inner Thigh
Three-position Calf Raise 122	1	10	1	15	2	25	Calves
Bent-over Twist 112	1	20	2	20	2	30	Waist & Hips
Alternate Upright Knee-in 108	1	10	1	20	2	20	Abdomen
Leg Raise & Circle 110	1	8	1	15	2	20	"
Stomach Firmer 113	1	8	1	15	2	20	"
Stomach Vacuum 114	1	3	1	5	1	5	"
Side Lateral Raise 131	1	10	1	15	1	25	Shoulder
Bent-over Laterals 132	1	10	1	15	1	25	Shoulder
Swan Lift 129	1	3	1	8	1	8	Back
Modified Push-ups 134	1	5	1	10	3	15	Chest
Neck Rolls 127	1	4	1	8	1	8	Neck
Relaxation							

GOOD MORNING

Purpose: This exercise will enable you to warm up your entire body by increasing your circulation and preparing you for the rest of your routine. This is one of my many favorite exercises because it also allows me to exercise that stubborn area right below the buttocks and above the leg bicep. The movement stretches your muscles, limbering and shaping your legs as it does.

Equipment: 5-foot wooden pole

Procedure: 1. Begin in the standing position. Your feet are about 18 inches apart with your knees slightly bent. Bending your knees will aid in the prevention of any unnecessary stress being placed on the lower back. 2. Place the pole across your shoulders, grasping it wherever it feels comfortable. 3. Take a deep breath through your nostrils and pull your buttocks and abdomen in very tight. 4. Slowly begin leaning forward and exhaling through your mouth until your upper body is parallel to the floor. Remember to keep your tummy pulled in. 5. After you reach parallel, take a deep breath as you begin rising up to your original start position. As you do this, pull your buttocks in tight and with concentration allow this area to help lift you up. 6. Recheck before doing your remaining repetitions. Is your body straight? Knees bent? Are you holding your tummy and buttocks in tightly?

SPINAL STRETCH

Purpose: This exercise warms up your body, preparing it for exercise. The spinal stretch is an excellent limbering movement which also stretches the spine and increases flexibility. Move slowly for best results.

Equipment: None

Procedure: 1. Standing, feet about 12 inches apart and knees slightly bent, clasp hands behind back and raise them as high as possible. 2. Slowly, keeping hands high, lean slightly back. Hold a few seconds. 3. Bend slowly forward until upper body is at a 90-degree angle to legs. Pull arms gently up over back. 4. Return to standing position and repeat. 5. Exhale as arms come up and inhale as you return to standing position. 6. To do the movement effectively, be sure to keep arms high, tummy in, and as you return to the standing position, tighten your buttocks. Move slowly. This is also an excellent way to firm a flabby rear end.

TRACK START

Purpose: This warm-up exercise not only helps shape your body but also helps increase your endurance. In only a matter of seconds your circulation will increase, warming your entire body. Pay careful attention that you are achieving maximum benefit from each movement because this exercise is wonderful for shaping the thighs and firming and lifting the buttocks.

Equipment: None

Procedure: 1. Begin this exercise with hands and knees on the floor. 2. Bring your right knee up to your chest, staying on your toes. Now, stretch your left leg straight back, with your weight resting on your toes. 3. Begin the movement by alternating your legs quickly, bringing the left leg forward and the right leg back. Continue repeating this movement at a rapid pace. 4. Exhale as the right leg comes forward. Inhale as the left leg comes forward. 5. Be sure you are keeping your leg straight and your tummy pulled in. Visualize your buttock and leg biceps muscles working as you do each repetition. This will improve your workout. Count only on the left leg.

STRADDLE SWING

Purpose: This exercise is a circulation stimulator which works your entire body. It also puts extra emphasis on firming your buttocks.

Equipment: None

Procedure: 1. Begin by standing with your hands clasped and stretched up over your head. Keep your feet approximately 2 feet apart and comfortable. Your toes should be pointing straight ahead. 2. Take a deep breath and then exhale as you swing your arms down, bending the knees slightly as you do. Push your arms through your legs forcefully. 3. Now pull your arms up as you inhale and straighten your legs back to the starting position. 4. Repeat at a moderate pace. 5. During the exercise concentrate on keeping your tummy tight and tensing your buttocks hard as you rise up into the standing position.

JUMPING JACKS

Purpose: This movement is a good, general all-over body toner which helps increase your circulation and warm up your body. Many people have a difficult time coordinating these movements but if they are done slowly at first, step by step, the rhythm can be picked up quickly. It is well worth the effort to perfect this.

Equipment: None

Procedure: 1. Begin in standing position, feet together, and hands close at sides. 2. Begin the movement with a hop by opening your legs and feet about 2½ feet apart while at the same time bringing your arms straight over your head with the backs of your hands together. 3. Hop again, returning to the start position. Do not land flat on your feet but on the toes first. 4. Inhale as you lift your arms and spread your legs. Exhale as you return to start position: Master the movement first and the breathing second if at first it seems difficult to do them together. 5. Be sure you keep your body stretched out. You will be amazed at the results on the waist and midriff area.

BODY STRETCH

Purpose: This warm-up exercise will enable you to increase your circulation rapidly. Be sure to follow the breathing pattern closely because this is also a fantastic way to increase your lung capacity when you inhale very deeply as you stretch your arms upward. As you bend forward you will feel the exercise working on the leg biceps (back of thighs) stretching, shaping and limbering.

Equipment: None

Procedure: Begin in standing position. Place your feet about six inches apart and have your hands down at your sides. 2. Inhale deeply and stretch your arms. Now stretch as high as you can with your right hand. At the same time lift up on your toes. 3. Now stretch a little further before you bring your feet flat on the floor. Keeping your arms straight, bend at the waist and touch your toes. Exhale as you go down. 4. The more advanced students should place the palms of their hands on the floor at this time. Those with weak lower backs should bend their knees slightly. 5. Keep your tummy in as you lift your body from toe touch to overhead and pull in your buttocks tightly. When you rise on your toes put your weight on the big toe. Do not allow your feet to roll over on their sides. 6. Now inhale deeply and stretch your arms as high as you can. This time stretch as high as you can with your left hand. You must stretch with both right and left hand before one rep is completed.

ALTERNATE UPRIGHT KNEE-IN

Purpose: In this upright leaning position your back is free from unnecessary strain. You will find this movement will flatten your tummy and tighten your buttocks, so be sure to do the full movement. Begin slowly at first and work up to a moderate pace. You will also find this movement can help strengthen a weak lower back.

Equipment: None

Procedure: 1. Begin in a seated position on the floor, leaning back on your arms, hands flat on the floor. Your right leg is extended straight out with your toes pointed and your left leg is bent at the knee and pulled toward your chest as far as it can go. Keep your feet approximately one to three inches from the floor. 2. Inhale deeply and then exhale as you extend your left leg and pull your right knee to your chest. 3. Each time your left knee comes to your chest it counts as one repetition. 4. Be sure to point and really stretch out the extended leg as well as pulling in the bent leg as close to your chest as possible.

LEG SPREAD TUMMY TRIMMER

Purpose: The primary purpose of this movement is to firm the abdomen but it also greatly benefits other body parts in the process. You will see results in strengthening your lower back as well as firming and shaping that hard-to-get area, the inner thigh. Be sure not to lower or lift your legs to ease any tension you feel in your abdomen. Keep the tension constant.

Equipment: None

Procedure: 1. Lie on your back and place your hands under your hips, palms down for support of your back. 2. Raise your legs to a distance of 1½ feet above the floor and hold them steady. Point your toes and inhale deeply. 3. Now, spread your legs as wide as possible, exhaling as you do. Repeat until you have done the desired amount of repetitions. Count repetitions each time your legs close. 4. Focus your attention on keeping the abdomen tense and the inner thighs tight. Allow the inner thigh to pull your legs closed.

LEG RAISE AND CIRCLE

Purpose: For firming the inner thighs, buttocks and most of all, the abdomen, this exercise is fantastic. The lower back will also benefit by gaining added strength. Keep close attention to your movements, getting the maximum benefit from each one.

Equipment: None

Procedure: 1. Begin by lying on your back. Place your hands under your hips for lower back support. Your legs should be straight out, toes pointed and feet raised about three inches from the floor. 2. Exhale and slowly raise your legs to a 90-degree angle. 3. Inhale as you spread your legs and circle them up and then back to starting position—three inches above the floor and together. This counts as one repetition. 4. Do the movements slowly, concentrating on your abdomen doing the work as you slowly raise and lower your legs. 5. To really work the inner thigh, stretch your legs by reaching with your toes and spreading wide your legs.

ALTERNATE ELBOW-TO-KNEE TWIST

Purpose: This exercise will work on reducing any excess flab at your waistline as well as on flattening and firming a not-so-firm-and-flat abdomen. Also, your circulation and your flexibility will increase. Begin slowly, and when you are familiar with the movement, work up to a moderate pace.

Equipment: None

Procedure: 1. Sit on the floor with your back straight. Clasp your hands behind your neck. 2. Bring your right knee up to a point slightly below your left elbow and extend your left leg, with the toes pointed, straight ahead, keeping your feet about 3 inches from the floor. Inhale. Twist your upper body so your left elbow comes near or touches your right knee. 3. Exhale and extend your right leg, bringing your left knee up a point slightly below your right elbow and twisting so as your right elbow touches your left knee. 4. Each time your right elbow touches your left knee, this is one repetition, and each time you return to this position, inhale. 5. Keep your movements exact and your legs stretched out. Concentrate on a tight abdomen and on your abdomen's doing the work of the movement.

BENT-OVER TWIST

Purpose: This is excellent for trimming both the waistline and the upper hips. Be sure to begin slowly and gradually build up speed, always remembering to keep your form in the movement correct.

Equipment: 5-foot wooden pole—or you may place your right hand on your right shoulder and your left hand on your left shoulder, pull your shoulders back and proceed with the movement.

Procedure: 1. Begin by standing with your feet about three feet apart. Place the pole across your shoulders and grip it comfortably at each end. 2. Bend at the waist, keeping your back flat and at a 90-degree angle to the legs. Your knees should stay slightly bent. 3. Keeping your hips and head stationary, begin twisting at the waist. Touch the left end of the bar to a point one inch above the floor slightly in front of your right foot. Then twist at the waist in the opposite direction so that the right end of the bar is about one inch above the floor, slightly in front of your left foot. This is one repetition. 5. For quickest results, concentrate on the movement and keep your tummy pulled in tight. For toning your legs at the same time, tighten your thighs throughout the movement.

STOMACH FIRMER

Purpose: This is a highly concentrated partial sit-up which gets right to the problem of firming the upper abdominal region and midriff, as well as strengthening a weak lower back. The partial movement keeps the abdomen tense and gives you twice the workout in half the time.

Equipment: None

Procedure: 1. Lie on your back with your knees bent and your feet flat on the floor. Place your hands across your chest. Inhale deeply. 2. Exhale as you lift only your head, shoulders, and upper back off the floor, curling your back as you do so. 3. Inhale as you return to start position. This is one repetition. 4. It is important not to try to do this with a straight back, but to keep it curved. Do not hold your breath. Concentrate on your breathing and on keeping your tummy tight. This exercise will tighten the buttocks as well as increase the firming effect on the abdomen. This may also be done with your feet resting on something elevated about one foot, perhaps a stool.

STOMACH VACUUM

Purpose: This exercise is great for trimming the abdomen and maintaining a supersmall waistline by allowing you to gain control over the abdominal muscles. This exercise should be done on an empty or near-empty stomach. It can give you amazing results in a very short time when done several times throughout each day.

Equipment: None

Procedure: 1. From a standing position bend over at the waist. Place your hands on your knees. 2. Exhale until all air is out of your lungs. Do not breathe in. Instead, suck your tummy in as far as you can—this should form a stomach vacuum. 3. Hold this position for ten seconds; try to hold it longer when you have had more practice. 4. Now relax and tense your abdominal muscles. Repeat. 5. If at first try you do not get a vacuum, you may not be exhaling all the air out of your lungs, or you may be taking a breath after you exhale. Try again. Mastering this movement is well worth the effort.

TWIST AND KICK

Purpose: Here is an exercise that not only tones your entire body and trims your hips and waist all at the same time, but also provides a great deal of fun. It really loosens you up.

Equipment: None

Procedure: 1. Begin by standing with your feet about six inches apart. Hold your arms straight out in front at shoulder level. 2. While doing the exercise follow this breathing pattern: Exhale as you twist to each side and inhale when your arms are straight out in front. 3. Begin the movement by twisting your upper body to the left and at the same time kicking your left leg to the right, causing the lower torso to twist to the right. 4. Now reverse and twist your upper body to the right and kick your right leg to the left side. This is one repetition. 5. While doing this exercise, be aware of your entire body. Keep your posture correct. Keeping your arms up at shoulder level and not allowing them to drop will help firm up the upper arms as well as help to keep your back straight. Remember, tummy in and toes pointed.

TRIM SITS

Purpose: To slim down to a tiny waistline and a firm midsection, follow this exercise's procedure closely. You will also begin to see some firming taking place in the buttocks and upper hips. Stretching to your maximum will give you long and more shapely muscles for the lean, trim look.

Equipment: None

Procedure: 1. Begin seated on your knees and heels. Clasp your hands together with the palms stretching upward, high over your head. 2. Lift your body to a kneeling position, inhaling as you do. 3. Now exhale as you sit with your weight on your left leg. Be sure to keep your arms stretched upward. 4. Next, inhale as you are returning to the kneeling position. 5. Exhale again and sit with your weight on your right leg. This is one repetition. 6. For a complete body workout keep your tummy in and always stretch as high as you can with your hands. This helps trim and firm your midriff as well as make the movement easier. By pulling your buttocks in during the up movement you will also be working the hips, buttocks and thighs.

ALTERNATE THIGH STRETCH

Purpose: This exercise will stretch the inner thigh of one leg as it stretches the alternate buttock and rear of the other legs. From practicing this movement your legs will be more shapely, your buttocks firmer and your body more supple. Do the exercise with very slow movements. Concentrate on the marvelous stretch you're getting and on a relaxed, yet stretched-out, back and spine.

Equipment: None

Procedure: 1. Begin seated on the floor, your back straight. Place the sole of your left foot against the upper inner thigh of the right leg. Be sure your right leg is stretched out in front of your body very tautly with the foot flexed—by that I mean pushing your heel out as you pull your toes back toward your body. Take a deep breath. 2. With your hands resting on your thigh, exhale, bending forward, and run your hands down your leg. Touch your forehead to your thigh and your fingers to your toes. 3. Inhale as you return to the upright position. 4. After all repetitions are completed on this leg, repeat the same movement on the left leg. 5. Keep your back straight. When your foot is flexed you automatically tense your legs, thus firming them. Keep aware of this and results will come faster.

KNEELING SIDE LEG LIFT

Purpose: Women usually hold a great deal of their excess fat on the outer part of the upper thigh. This area can only be worked on effectively with exercises specifically designed for it. This exercise I have found to be extremely effective in combating the problem. It will both firm and reduce the outer thigh as well as work on the hips and buttocks.

Equipment: None, unless you need something under your knees as a cushion.

Procedure: 1. From a position on your hands and knees, extend your right leg straight out to the side and point your toes. Take a deep breath. 2. Now exhale and raise your right leg high up to the side keeping it straight and tensed. 3. Inhale and lower the leg to about one inch above the floor. This is one repetition. 4. Continue repeating the movement, concentrating on raising and lowering the leg slowly, and feeling the tension in the leg, thigh and buttocks. 5. Keep your foot flexed and pulled up to the side position. Repeat with other leg.

KNEELING KNEE TO CHEST

Purpose: I have always included this exercise in my training. I find it to be one of the most effective for the area between the buttocks and the leg biceps. Excellent for lifting, firming and shaping sagging buttocks, at the same time benefiting the thighs and hips.

Equipment: None, or three-pound ankle weights

Procedure: 1. Begin on your hands and knees. Looking down, inhale deeply. 2. Now exhale as you point your right toe and extend your right leg back up as far as possible. 3. Inhale and bring your right knee up toward your chest. This is one repetition. 4. Continue the repetitions on the right leg keeping that knee from touching the floor. Next do the repetitions on the left leg. 5. During the movement keep your legs tense and lift your leg as high as you can. Concentrate on keeping the buttocks and tummy tight and the leg biceps raising the leg.

LEG SPREAD AND CROSS

Purpose: This exercise will work both the inner and outer thigh. When your legs cross you're working the outer thigh, and when you spread your legs you work the inner thigh. Therefore you will want to work equally hard on completing both movements for firmer and more shapely thighs.

Equipment: None

Procedure: 1. Lying on your back, place your hands under your hips for support. With your legs held together lift them straight up to form a 90-degree angle. 2. Inhale as you spread your legs wide. You may either flex or point your toes. 3. Exhale and keep your legs straight as you cross them (left over right). You may have to bend them ever so slightly. 4. Open your legs to spread position, inhaling. This is one repetition. Repeat, this time crossing right leg over left. 5. If you really push your legs open you will be working the inner thighs. Pushing across will be working the outer thighs. Naturally, keep your tummy tight throughout the movement.

HEEL CLICKS

Purpose: Sometimes this is a hard one to get going on but it is a super exercise to master. Even when you are still attempting to perfect this movement you are getting a super workout. But when you master it you won't believe how fantastic this exercise really is for firming and lifting your buttocks. The spinal erector muscles that run along the sides of your spine will increase their strength also, making for a very healthy back.

Equipment: None

Procedure: 1. Lie on your tummy and place your hands under your pelvis for support and cushion. Lift both of your legs together off the floor as high as you possibly can. 2. Keeping the legs held very high, inhale as you open them wide, and exhale as you bring your heels together. Do all repetitions at a moderate speed. 3. Always concentrate on keeping your legs straight, your feet flexed and high, and your buttocks tight. Don't allow your legs to drop.

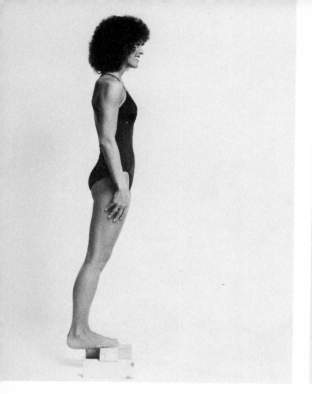

THREE-POSITION CALF RAISE

Purpose: This calf movement will firm and shape the entire calf area. Both calves are worked at the same time, and by changing your foot positions you will be able to work front, back, inside and outside of your calf. This movement may also be done on one leg at a time by balancing on one foot. This gives more weight resistance on the calf.

Equipment: Calf block

Procedure: 1. Begin by standing with your feet one foot apart. Your knees may be locked or slightly bent. 2. To work the back of the calf, keep your toes facing forward and exhale, rising up on your toes, and inhale as you lower to start position. 3. To work the outer part of your calf, point your toes inward and rise and lower on your toes again. 4. To work the inside of your calf, point toes out and rise and lower on your toes. 5. Do all your repetitions for one position before moving on to the next position. 6. Do not neglect the rest of your body. Be sure to stand erect with your shoulders held back and down. For a firm hip area, also hold your tummy and buttocks in tight. (See men's section for closeups.)

REAR LEG LIFT

Purpose: This exercise primarily firms your buttocks but it also can help to firm and strengthen a weak back. The movement should be done slowly and deliberately. You should control the movement throughout the entire exercise.

Equipment: None, unless you wish a cushion under your pelvic area

Procedure: 1. Lying on your stomach, place your hands under your pelvis for support and cushion. 2. Begin with your right leg and exhale as you lift your right leg straight up and high. 3. Inhale and slowly lower the leg. 4. Point your toes and keep your body flat on the floor. Stretch the leg as you lift and lower. 5. Do all repetitions on the right leg before beginning on the left. 6. Be sure you tighten your buttocks and keep your leg straight. Concentrate on your leg and let it do all the lifting. Do not bounce your leg off the floor. Instead, *lift* it very slowly.

SIDE LEG CIRCLES

Purpose: This limbering and loosening movement will help reduce fat accumulation on the outer thigh, inner thigh, hips and buttocks and will also firm these. If your circles are nice and wide you will also be working your waistline, trimming it down.

Equipment: None

Procedure: 1. Lie on your side and bend your bottom leg at the knee for support. Place one hand on the floor in front of you and the other under your head. Keep your top leg completely straight with the foot flexed. 2. Next, exhale as you pull your leg out in front of your body in a circular pattern, out and upward. 3. Inhale now as you pull your leg to the back and circle it back to the start position. This one large circle you have made with your leg is one repetition. Complete all repetitions on this leg before changing and working the other leg. 4. Keeping your foot flexed and your leg straight will help to tighten and firm your buttocks and thighs. Try to remain lying on your side—do not allow your body to roll to the front or back.

LEG OVERS

Purpose: This waist and hip slimmer is super-effective when the procedure is followed closely. As well as slimming your waistline, it also increases your flexibility in this area. For greater relaxation, do this movement with your eyes closed and your concentration on your breath and on your waistline.

Equipment: None

Procedure: 1. Lie on your back and stretch your arms out to your sides at a 90-degree angle. Place your legs straight out, resting on the floor, and together. 2. Inhale as you lift your right leg up very high, keeping it straight. When your leg is as high as you can get it, pull it over to your left side as close as you can get to your hand. 3. Exhale and return the leg to the starting position. 4. Repeat with your left leg, alternating between right and left. Count repetitions on your left leg only. 5. Keep your toes pointed and your legs held tight and straight. The upper body, especially the shoulders, should be kept very flat to the floor. This will give your waistline and hips a very good workout.

INNER THIGH STRETCH

Purpose: Even if you have a difficult time with this one, you should definitely work on mastering it because you probably need to limber and stretch the inner thigh muscles. Begin slowly and gradually increase your pace. It is excellent for firming and shaping your inner thighs and for giving your legs added flexibility.

Equipment: None

Procedure: 1. Begin by sitting upright with your back straight and the soles of your feet together and pulled in as close to your body as possible. Hold on to your toes and place your elbows on your knees. Lean forward keeping your shoulders back and your back straight. It

will feel as though you are reaching with your chest to touch your feet.
2. Exhale, keep your back straight and lean forward over your feet with
your elbows pushing on your knees gently. 3. Inhale and allow your
knees to come up slightly. Repeat, each time pushing out a little farther.
4. You will get a better stretch if you pull up on your toes as you push
down with your elbows. Begin slowly and increase your pace gradually
to a moderate rhythm.

NECK ROLLS

Purpose: This exercise should be done slowly and with your
full attention on the movement. Close your eyes as you do this exercise
and become aware of the stretching and relaxing that is taking place.
This is also a good way to tone up and strengthen your neck.

Equipment: None

Procedure: 1. Be seated in a comfortable position and hold your
head erect with your shoulders relaxed. Inhale. 2. Allow your head to
drop slowly and easily to your right shoulder, exhaling as you roll
your neck and chin toward your chest. Now circle up to the left side
and begin dropping your head back. 3. After one complete circle,
stop and inhale, then circle in the opposite direction. 4. Completely
relax your head, facial muscles, shoulders and neck. Breathe deeply
and move slowly.

SHOULDER SHRUG AND CIRCLE

Purpose: This movement will increase flexibility in your shoulders and relax them by relieving any stored tension you might be holding in this area. Close your eyes and breathe very deeply, keeping your concentration centered on your breath and your slow, deliberate movements.

Equipment: None

Procedure: 1. Sitting cross-legged, bring your hands to rest on your upper thighs. 2. Inhale and lift your shoulders as high as you can. Keep your arms relaxed. Hold this position for a count of five. 3. Now exhale and circle your shoulders back and down, and around to shrug position again. This is one repetition. 4. Be sure to keep your back straight, but not tense. Continue relaxing and releasing tension from your shoulders and upper back with each breath.

SWAN LIFT

Purpose: This exercise will work your entire body. It is effective in firming and strengthening your lower back, shaping up your mid-section and increasing your total body flexibility. Do all repetitions slowly and completely.

Equipment: None, unless you need a cushion for pelvis

Procedure: 1. Lie on your stomach and grasp your ankles with your hands. Keep your head up. 2. Now inhale and pull up on your ankles, lifting your head high and arching your back at the same time. 3. Exhale and very slowly relax back into start position. This is one repetition. 4. Pull up and arch your back very slowly and high, yet not straining. Stay in complete control of this exercise by concentrating deeply on every move.

ARM CIRCLES

Purpose: If you wish to have firmer arms, shoulders and upper back, this movement will assist you in attaining just that. Your arms may tire at first but don't give in. Keep your arms up and held tight. In just a short period of time you will be seeing results in firmer and more shapely arms.

Equipment: None

Procedure: 1. Standing with your feet about 18 inches apart (or together, if you wish, as long as you feel balanced and comfortable), extend your arms straight out to each side, holding the palms of your hands upward. 2. Throughout this exercise breathe long and deep, inhaling and exhaling the maximum each time. 3. Begin the movement by moving your straight-held arms in very small circles and gradually increasing the size of the circles to very large. Reverse the direction of your circles every 20 repetitions. 4. Concentrate on controlling your movements by your shoulders and upper arms. 5. Remember to keep good posture; pull your buttocks in and hold your tummy tight—you can also profit from doing this by firming your hips, and buttocks and waist. Keep your shoulders relaxed and held back.

SIDE LATERAL RAISE

Purpose: For beautiful shapely shoulders, do this exercise. I love it. It firms and shapes the arms, back and shoulders, and the results show quickly.

Equipment: None

Procedure: 1. Stand with your feet 18 inches apart (or together —whichever gives most stability and comfort) and place your hands down at your sides. 2. Inhale and, raising your arms over your head, touch the backs of your hands together. 3. Very slowly exhale as you lower your arms to the starting position. 4. Concentrate on your breath, keeping your body in good posture, with your tummy in and your buttocks tight. Do the movement slowly. The body should remain stationary and the arms straight.

BENT-OVER LATERALS

Purpose: When I am beginning to feel tired and as though I am carrying a tremendous load on my shoulders, causing me to slump over, I find this exercise of great assistance and relief. It is excellent for the upper back, shoulders and arms, firming, shaping and reducing any excess fat.

Equipment: None

Procedure: 1. Standing with your feet apart or together, whichever is most comfortable for you, bend over at the waist, holding your arms straight down with the palms of your hands together. Inhale. 2. Exhale and slowly raise your straight-held arms as high as possible. Do not force the movement. 3. Inhale and slowly return your arms to the start position. 4. Keep your back straight. Move slowly throughout the exercise. Do not rise until you have completed the exercise.

MODIFIED PUSH-UPS

Purpose: To keep your chest and arms firm do this movement slowly. Concentrate not only on pushing your arms but also on your chest. Tense your chest with each movement.

Equipment: None

Procedure: 1. Get down on your hands and knees. Rest on your hands, which are placed shoulder distance apart, with the fingers pointing inward. Keep your knees on the floor and lift your feet and calves off the floor. 2. Inhale and slowly lower your upper body to the floor. Bend only the elbows. Keep your waist and back straight. Touch only your chin to the floor. 3. Now, to rise, exhale as you push your body to the starting position. This is one repetition. 4. For best results do not rest on the floor, and keep your body straight.

8 · Exercising with Weights

This section is devoted to the woman who wishes to use resistance exercises in her training. The equipment utilized here is basic and very effective. I have found that the more basic, simple and uncomplicated a movement is, the more effective it seems to be. You can master such movements much more quickly; thus results come more quickly, too.

Weight training enables you in an efficient, quick way to begin shaping, building or reducing your present body. As you use heavier weights you will see your body becoming more shapely and feel it becoming firmer in a short period of time. These exercises are easily done at home or at a gym, with only a minimum of equipment. Begin these routines by trying each exercise movement with little or no weight to familiarize yourself with the exercise and to get your form correct. Form (how the movement is performed) is very important here. Follow the directions found with the exercise descriptions, and the photos, very closely.

These routines are, again as in the free form exercises, divided into 3 major routines: Basic, Middle, and Success, and within each routine there are divisions for levels of difficulty: Beginner, Intermediate, Advanced. (Refer back to page 96 for how to progress within your program.) As with the free form routines, these routines with weights should be practiced three times weekly on alternate days.

Basic Routine

This first routine is a very basic one for those who have never trained with weights or who have done very little exercise at all. The emphasis is on giving you a very good general body-conditioning routine for firming and shaping up. As with all programs, follow in the order set down. You will find the amount of weight to be used, how many times you repeat the complete exercise (sets), and how many times you repeat the movement (reps).

BASIC ROUTINE

EXERCISE/PAGE	BE-GINNER			INTER-MEDIATE			AD-VANCED			Purpose
	weight	*sets*	*reps*	*weight*	*sets*	*reps*	*weight*	*sets*	*reps*	
Mental Preparation										
Dumbbell Swing 140	2	1	8	5	1	10	5	1	15	Warm-up
Incline Flys 144	3	1	10	5	1	10	8	1	12	Chest
Pullovers 146	3	1	8	5	1	10	8	2	10	Upper Body
Press Behind Neck 147	10	1	5	10	1	10	12	1	12	Shoulder/ Back
One-arm Tricep Extensions 149	3	1	8	3	1	10	3	1	15	Triceps
Stiff-legged Leg Lift 152	0	1	10	3	2	10	3	2	15	Thighs
Kneeling Knee to Chest 119	0	1	15	3	2	8	3	2	15	"
Heel Clicks 121	0	1	10	0	2	20	3	1	15	Buttocks
Seated Twist 158	0	1	15	0	2	30	0	2	50	Waist
Leg Raise (Bench) 157	0	1	10	0	2	15	0	2	20	Tummy
Relaxation										

Note: You may need more or less weight depending on your strength.

Middle Routine

The next routine is a good basic routine emphasizing all body parts. The chest portion of the routine comes first and works on building and firming your bustline to give it more support and shape and at the same time reduces excess fat from the back and chest area. The exercises in this portion also do a great deal for proper body alignment and correcting posture problems. You will also find through doing these movements your arms will become firmer and more shapely, and with no, or very little, increase in size.

The second portion of the routine concentrates on hips, thighs, buttocks and calves. You will find a wide variety of movements here to help firm and shape your lower body as well as reduce ugly fat from outer thighs and hips—an area where many women pack on those unnecessary pounds.

Last, you will find a portion of the program devoted entirely to giving you the trim, attractive midsection which is necessary to tie in your upper and lower body and create a total appearance that is pleasing. Your midsection is worked last, when your stomach is its emptiest and allows you more freedom of movement; at that time you have, as well, an already warmed-up lower back and abdomen area after having performed other movements in the other areas.

Listed as follows are the exercise, the amount of weight, and the number of times recommended for doing the movement for best results at all three levels of difficulty.

MIDDLE ROUTINE

EXERCISE/PAGE	BE-GINNER			INTER-MEDIATE			AD-VANCED			Purpose
	weight	*sets*	*reps*	*weight*	*sets*	*reps*	*weight*	*sets*	*reps*	
Mental Preparation										
Clean & Press 142	0	1	10	10	2	8	12	2	10	Warm-up
Incline Fly 144	5	1	8	10	2	12	15	3	12	Upper Body
Decline Fly 145	5	1	8	10	2	12	15	3	12	" "
Pullovers 146	5	1	8	10	2	12	15	3	15	" "
Press Behind Neck 147	10	1	10	12	2	10	12	2	15	" "
Bent-over Kick Back 148	2	1	20	4	1	20	5	1	25	Arms
Bent-over Rowing 150	10	1	8	12	1	15	15	1	15	Back
Leg Lunge 151	5	1	8	10	1	10	10	1	15	Legs
Kneeling Knee to Chest 119	3	1	10	3	2	15	3	2	25	"
Leg Extension 154	3	1	8	3	1	10	3	1	15	"
Stiff-legged Leg Lift 152	0	1	6	3	1	10	3	2	15	"
Three-position Calf Raise 155	5	1	10	10	1	15	15	1	15	"
Knee to Chest (Bench) 156	0	1	10	0	1	20	0	2	25	Abdomen
Leg Raise (Bench) 157	0	1	10	0	1	20	0	2	25	"
Seated Twist 158	0	1	50	0	1	75	0	2	75	Waist
Bent-over Twist 112	0	1	20	0	1	40	0	1	50	"
Stomach Firmer 113	0	1	8	0	1	10	0	2	15	Abdomen
Relaxation										

Success Routine

The Success Routine is especially for the woman who has been training with weights regularly (*at least* three times per week) and wants to set up her program for quicker and more effective results.

The routine that follows gives weight exercises which help firm and shape the body as well as rid it of excess fat. Here the main emphasis is on the legs: trimming down and shaping, as well as creating stronger, healthier legs. Be sure to follow the entire routine in the order in which it is laid out for achieving the most effective results.

SUCCESS ROUTINE

EXERCISE/PAGE	BE-GINNER			INTER-MEDIATE			AD-VANCED			Purpose
	weight	*sets*	*reps*	*weight*	*sets*	*reps*	*weight*	*sets*	*reps*	
Mental Preparation										
Dumbbell Swing 140	3	1	10	5	1	15	8	2	10	Warm-ups
Good Morning 101	0	1	10	10	1	15	15	2	10	"
Leg Lunge 151	5	1	10	10	1	15	12	2	20	Legs
Front Leg Lift 153	0	1	10	3	1	15	3	2	20	"
Three-position Calf Raise 155	8	1	10	10	2	10	15	2	15	"
Incline Fly 144	5	1	10	10	2	12	15	3	15	Upper Body
Decline Fly 145	5	1	10	10	2	12	15	3	15	"
Pullover 146	5	1	10	10	2	12	15	3	15	"
Press Behind Neck 147	10	1	12	12	2	15	15	2	15	"
Bent-over Rowing 150	10	1	12	15	2	15	20	2	15	Back
One-arm Tricep Extensions 149	3	1	10	5	2	15	8	2	15	Arms
Alternate Elbow to Knee 111	0	1	10	0	1	20	0	2	20	Abdomen
Leg Raise (Bench) 157	1	1	10	1	1	20	0	2	20	"
Knee to Chest (Bench) 156	0	1	10	0	1	20	0	2	20	"
Seated Twist 158	0	1	50	0	2	50	0	2	100	Waist
Bent-over Twist 112	0	1	20	0	2	20	0	2	35	"
Stomach Vacuum 114	0	1	6	0	1	10	0	1	10	"
Relaxation										

DUMBBELL SWING

Purpose: The advantages of this exercise are many. Primarily you will be using this movement to get your body warmed up and ready to work out. It is a circulation stimulator; in addition, it works on your entire body, especially firming your rear end.

Equipment: One lightweight dumbbell. Check your chart for the correct weight to use.

Procedure: 1. In a standing position, place your feet approximately 2½ feet apart. The legs should be spread, yet comfortable. Hold the dumbbell with both hands and raise your arms over your head. Inhale deeply, lifting your rib cage and expanding your lungs to capacity. 2. Exhale as you swing the dumbbell down through your legs, bending your knees slightly as you do. Push back past your heels. 3. Now inhale and swing the dumbbell, still keeping your arms straight, over your head, returning to starting position with lungs expanded fully. 4. Remember to tuck your buttocks in as you swing up, and, of course, always keep a tight, flat abdomen.

GOOD MORNING (see photo on page 102)

Purpose: You will be using this movement primarily for warming up the muscles, but don't forget it is also excellent for strengthening the lower back and giving a marvelous stretch and firming to the area between the buttocks and leg biceps.

Equipment: A lightweight bar. Check your chart for the proper amount of weight to use.

Procedure: 1. Standing with your back straight and your feet resting firmly on the floor approximately 12 inches apart, place a lightweight bar across your shoulders, gripping it with both hands about 12 inches out from each shoulder. Inhale. 2. Exhale and bend forward from the waist, keeping the back straight and knees unlocked. Bend no lower than 90 degrees from your legs. 3. When you reach this 90-degree angle, begin lifting up again, as you inhale, and tuck your buttocks under. This is one repetition. 4. Remember to lift with your buttocks and back. Try not to rest your arms on the bar, thus causing unnecessary weight on the shoulders. Grip the bar lightly.

CLEAN AND PRESS

Purpose: You will be using this exercise mainly as a warm-up movement to ready your body for the rest of your routine, but it holds other benefits also. For one thing your shoulders will become stronger and more shapely. You will notice an improvement in your posture, and you will tighten up your buttocks. Establish a moderate rhythm as you do this movement. Use only an extremely light weight when performing it.

Equipment: Check your chart for the right weight bar to use. If this weight is too heavy to allow you to complete the movement properly, choose a lighter one that you can handle easily.

Procedure: 1. Stand with your feet about 18 inches apart and with the bar centered on the floor in front of your feet. Inhale. 2. Exhale and partially squat (with your knees bent); your hands gripping the bar should be about 2½ feet apart. 3. Inhale as you lift your body straight up, keeping your arms down and rising with your knees as you raise your back. Keep your buttocks tight. 4. When you are upright, posture correct, pull the bar to your upper chest and then, exhaling, push or press the weight over your head. Do not curve your back. 5. Inhale as you lower the weight to your chest. 6. Now exhale and place the weight on the floor, bending your knees into a partial squat as you do. This is one repetition. 7. Follow the procedure closely and refer to the photos as guides.

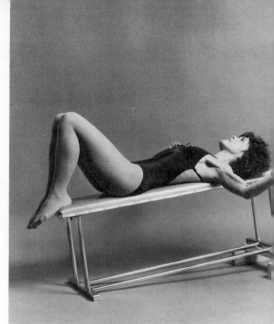

INCLINE FLY

Purpose: This excellent exercise will firm your chest muscles and lift a sagging bustline. Being on an incline allows you to work on the area just above your bustline—your upper chest. You will develop a cleavage if you have none or you will firm and shape an already existing cleavage. Your arms will also improve their shape with this movement—but be sure not to grasp the weight tightly. Instead, cradle the weight in a loose, open hand.

Equipment: Two dumbbells (check your routine for the correct weight) and an incline bench set at a 45-degree angle.

Procedure: 1. Sit on the end of the incline bench and pick up the dumbbells. Lean back on the incline and raise the dumbbells over your chest. Hold the dumbbells with open hands and insides of your wrists facing each other. Slightly unlock your elbows. 2. Now inhale and keep your elbows bent as you pull your arms open and down, below shoulder level. 3. Concentrate on your chest muscles as they help push the weights back to your starting position, while you exhale completely. 4. Do the movements slowly. It is important to keep your elbows out to the side if you are interested in building your bustline. Use a weight you are able to control, yet which offers a great deal of resistance. If you wish to lose inches from your bustline, use a light weight and increase the number of repetitions you do.

DECLINE FLY

Purpose: Here is a very effective chest exercise that will produce pleasing results. After practicing this exercise for only a short period of time, you will notice your bust lifting, firming and having more shape. Concentrate on your chest, allowing the chest muscles to help push the weight over your body. Concentrating on the area will give you more control over the exercise, thus better results.

Equipment: A flat bench raised to a low incline of about 10 to 15 degrees (a calf block can be used for this purpose). You also need two dumbbells (check your routine for the weight). If you wish to firm and shape, follow your routine. If you wish to build your bustline, use a weight heavier than that suggested, which will give you more resistance, yet one you can still control. If you wish to reduce the size of your bust, do more repetitions and keep the weight relatively light.

Procedure: 1. Sit on the raised edge of the bench. Lift dumbbells and lie back down the decline, raising dumbbells over your chest and raising your legs with knees bent. Hold dumbbells loosely with open hands, wrists facing each other. 2. Inhale as you open your arms out to the sides, bending your elbows slightly. Bring the dumbbells down and a little past shoulder level. Always keep your elbows out— do not squeeze them in toward your body. 3. With complete concentration on your tense chest muscles, push the dumbbells over your body, returning them to the starting position as you exhale. 4. Do the repetitions very slowly. Be in complete control of your weights and your movements.

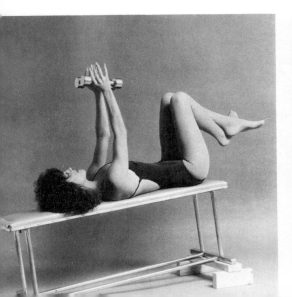
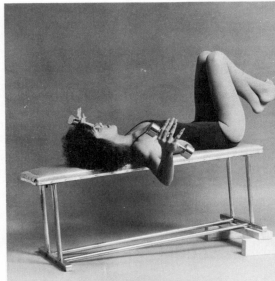

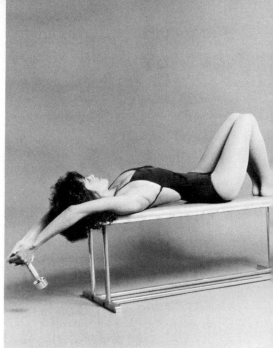

PULLOVERS

Purpose: This movement is fantastic for increasing lung capacity, lifting the rib cage, firming the midsection, firming and shaping the upper arms and trimming the waistline. The stretch feels fabulous and should be done very slowly. Your breathing pattern is very important in helping you attain your results; follow it carefully.

Equipment: You will need a flat bench and a dumbbell of proper weight (check your routine).

Procedure: 1. Lie on the bench, holding the dumbbell with both hands over your chest. Your knees should be bent and your feet flat on the bench. This will take any unnecessary stress or pressure off the lower back. 2. Slowly take a deep, deep breath, and with your arms slightly unlocked begin dropping your arms back and below the level of your head. Your rib cage should expand and lift upward. 3. Now begin exhaling and at the same time lift your arms up to just above your head. Do not return completely to your starting position. Keep constant tension on the muscles involved in this movement. 4. Move slowly. Breathe deeply. Keep your body loose and relaxed.

PRESS BEHIND NECK

Purpose: This movement is used to firm, shape and strengthen the shoulders, upper back, upper chest and arms. This exercise will also improve your posture.

Equipment: You will need a lightweight bar (check your routine for the proper weight).

Procedure: 1. Stand to do this exercise. Place your feet about 12 inches apart. Place the light bar across your shoulders, gripping it with loose, open hands at shoulder's width. Keep your elbows back. 2. Exhale as you press the weight fully over your head. 3. Next, inhale as you slowly lower the bar to your shoulders—but remember not to rest the weight on your shoulders; continue your repetitions. 4. To give your buttocks and waist a little workout, keep them held tight.

BENT-OVER KICK BACK

Purpose: If you have been careless about your diet or you are not getting enough exercise for your upper arms, you may find yourself storing some excess fat on the backs of the upper arms (the triceps). This exercise will take care of that problem by firming up and shaping that area. Your rear shoulder muscles will also profit by firming from this movement.

Equipment: You will need two lightweight dumbbells (check your routine for proper weight).

Procedure: 1. This exercise is done standing with your feet 12 inches apart. Bend over at the waist. Your arms are bent and held close to the body. Lift your elbows up high in the back. Hold one dumbbell in each hand and close to the bustline. 2. Exhale as you push your forearms back and up, always keeping your arms in close. 3. Now inhale and return to start position. 4. One more reminder: It is very important to keep your elbows in close to your body and up high in the back. For an added workout, keep the buttocks and tummy tensed.

ONE-ARM TRICEP EXTENSIONS

Purpose: This exercise will help firm and shape up a sagging tricep (the back of your upper arm). Concentrate on getting a good stretch and feeling the muscle tensing and relaxing.

Equipment: You will need one lightweight dumbbell (check your routine).

Procedure: 1. Stand with a straight back and relaxed shoulders. Holding the dumbbell in your right hand, raise your right arm straight over your head, pulling your elbow back and keeping it close to your head. Inhale. Now lower the dumbbell down to the back of your neck. Keep your elbow back. This is your starting position. 2. Now exhale and push the dumbbell overhead. 3. Inhale and slowly lower the dumbbell back to your starting position.

BENT-OVER ROWING

Purpose: This exercise will help you develop a pleasing taper to your upper body, causing your waist to appear smaller. You will also begin to notice your spinal erector muscles, which run along each side of the spine, becoming stronger, thus giving more support to your back. Do the movement slowly.

Equipment: One bar, fairly light in weight. Check your chart for appropriate weight.

Procedure: 1. Stand with your feet placed about two feet apart. Bend over at the waistline and keep your back straight with knees bent slightly. Grip the bar gently, keeping your hands about 2½ feet apart. Let your arms hang straight. Inhale. 2. Exhale as you pull the bar up to your chest. As you bend your elbows keep them pointed straight out to the sides. Do not lift your back during the movement. 3. Now, inhale and slowly lower the weight until your arms are again straight. 4. Concentrate on your back, especially the latissimus dorsi muscles (located on each side of the back). For an added workout, pull your buttocks and tummy in and hold them tight.

LEG LUNGE

Purpose: This exercise is particularly helpful in strengthening your thighs and knees; it also firms and lifts your buttocks and stretches and shapes your thigh muscles, creating long, lovely legs. Your balance will also improve.

Equipment: You will need two dumbbells; be sure to check your chart for the correct weight.

Procedure: 1. Begin by standing with your left foot placed one giant step ahead of your right. Depending on your leg length, this will be approximately a distance of three feet. Hold one dumbbell in each hand. Let your arms hang to your sides. The weight will give you added resistance to the movement. 2. Inhale and lunge forward on the left leg, bending the left knee as you do. The only movement you should have in your feet will be the right heel lifting slightly off the floor. Keep your right leg straight and your back straight as well. 3. Next, exhale and, pushing with your left leg, lift back up to the starting position. Remember, do not move your feet. This is one repetition.

STIFF-LEGGED LEG LIFT

Purpose: You will feel the effects of this movement immediately and you will see the results in a very short time. This exercise will firm and reduce your outer thighs, hips and buttocks. Concentrate on lifting your leg from the outer thigh. I think you will be pleased with the results of this exercise.

Equipment: You will need a pair of lightweight ankle weights not over three pounds each.

Procedure: 1. Lying on your left side, use your left hand to prop your head up. Now bend your left knee so as to support your body and keep it still during the exercise. Bring your right leg straight out in front of your body until it is at a 90-degree angle to your upper body. 2. Holding your leg in this position, exhale and lift your right leg as high as you can. Be sure to keep the 90-degree angle. 3. Next, exhale and lower your leg to just above the floor. This is one repetition. 4. At first you may wish to do this exercise without weights to help you familiarize yourself with the movement and gain better control.

FRONT LEG LIFT

Purpose: The primary purpose of this exercise is to firm, shape and remove any excess fat from the thighs. The movement will also work the buttocks and help firm the leg biceps. Do the movement slowly, concentrating on keeping the thighs and buttocks tightened.

Equipment: You will need a pair of lightweight ankle weights, not more than three pounds each.

Procedure: 1. Standing with good posture and with your feet together, pull your buttocks and tummy in tight. You may hold onto a chair or hold your arms out to each side for balance—or if your balance is good, you may poise your arms in any comfortable standing position. 2. Now lift your right leg very slowly. Exhale as you lift and be sure to keep your toes pointed and your thigh tense. Bring your leg up until parallel to the floor. 3. Next inhale and ever so slowly lower your leg. Be sure you keep the leg straight as you lower back into starting position. This is one repetition. 4. Do all repetitions for the right leg before going on to the left. At first you may wish to try the exercise without the ankle weights to become familiar with the movement.

LEG EXTENSIONS

Purpose: This exercise can also be done on a specially built piece of equipment designed for the specific purpose of doing leg extensions. However, not too many people have access to a leg-extension table; therefore I will show you how you can do a similar movement using ankle weights to take its place. The exercise is excellent for firming and shaping your thighs, as well as tightening your buttocks.

Equipment: Lightweight (three-pound) ankle weights

Procedure: 1. Standing with your feet together and your hands on your hips, lift your right knee until your thigh is parallel to the floor. Inhale. 2. Exhale as you extend your foot forward as far as you can, toes pointed out. 3. Now inhale and bring your foot back. This is one repetition. 4. Repeat the same movement on the left leg after you have completed all repetitions on the right leg. 4. For a very good workout, keep your posture correct, your tummy tight, your knee parallel to the floor, and your toes pointed.

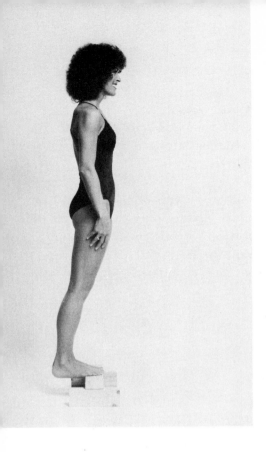 

THREE-POSITION CALF RAISE

Purpose: This exercise will firm and shape the entire calf area. If you wish to build your calf, then you should continually increase the amount of weight you use.

Equipment: You will need a calf block and a set of dumbbells to give you added resistance on this movement.

Procedure: 1. Stand with your feet placed about 12 inches apart, toes and balls of the feet resting on the edge of the calf block. Let your heels drop down as far as possible. Keep your knees locked. 2. To work the back of the calf, keep your toes facing forward. Holding a dumbbell in each hand, exhale as you rise on your toes and slowly lower as you inhale. Do all of your repetitions together for each foot position. 3. To work the outer part of your calf, point your toes in and rise and lower on your toes. 4. To work the inside of your calf, point your toes out and rise and lower on your toes. Do these movements slowly.

KNEE TO CHEST (BENCH)

Purpose: This exercise trims and flattens your abdomen. You will also notice your lower back becoming stronger from this movement.

Equipment: A flat bench

Procedure: 1. Begin by sitting on an end of the bench. Lean back with slightly bent elbows, hands firmly gripping each side of the bench. 2. Inhale, bringing your knees up to your chest, toes pointed. 3. Exhale as you push your feet toward the floor. 4. This is one repetition. Continue until all repetitions are completed. 5. Keep your abdomen held in tightly.

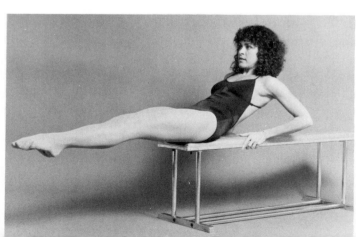

LEG RAISE

Purpose: With this exercise you will be working your lower abdomen—this is the area just below your waistline. Do this movement slowly, keeping the area tense throughout the exercise.

Equipment: For this exercise you will need a flat bench, a block of wood to prop it up, and, if you wish (advanced students only) some added resistance. In that case, wear three-pound ankle weights.

Procedure: 1. Prop the bench up slightly at one end. Lie on the bench with your head on the incline so that if you were to sit up your buttocks would hang slightly over the end. Hold onto the bench as pictured. Your legs should be straight out. 2. Exhale and slowly lower your legs as far as you can. 3. Inhale as you raise your legs until they are even with your abdomen—do not raise them any higher. You want to keep constant tension on your abdomen. Do all repetitions with no pause.

SEATED TWIST

Purpose: This exercise will trim and firm your waist and help lower back and upper hips to look slimmer and more attractive. When the twist is done on a bench it greatly concentrates the effects on the waistline. This movement should be done slowly at first and gradually worked up to a faster pace. This allows the waist and back to become warmed up.

Equipment: For this exercise you will need a lightweight five-foot wooden pole and a flat bench.

Procedure: 1. Straddle the bench and lock your feet around the legs of the bench. Rest the pole, centered, across your shoulders, gripping it gently out near the ends, wherever you feel comfortable. Keep your back and head straight. Focus your eyes on a point straight in front of you. Do not move your hips or legs. Inhale and twist your upper body to the right as far as you can. 2. Now exhale and twist fully to the left. This is one repetition. Continue all repetitions without pause.

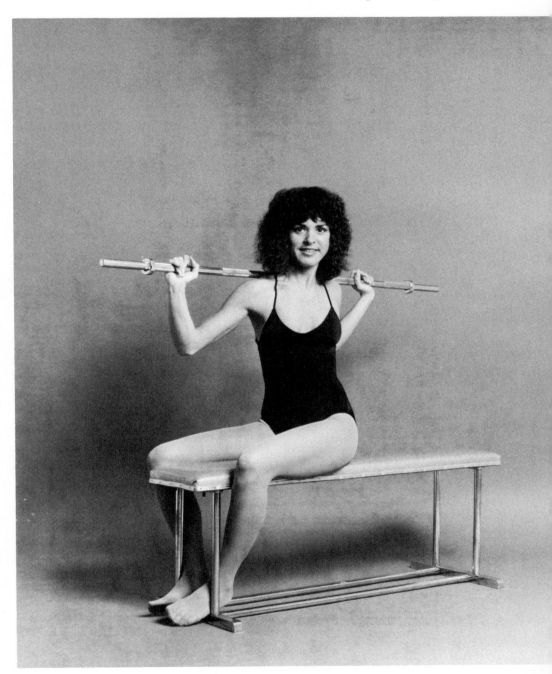

RESULTS

How long will it take before you have *visible results?* If you follow your program regularly for a period of four to six weeks you will begin to see results. Not everyone's body responds to exercise in the same way—therefore others will be slower or faster than you. Don't get discouraged and quit. Remember how long it has taken you to get out of shape. A slow, regular program will produce lasting results. When you shape up slowly, whether you're reducing or gaining, you will be able to remain in this great condition longer than if you had "crashed" to get there. When this program is followed gradually and progressively it becomes a way of life. Do not let a little fatigue keep you from exercising—this may be exactly what you need. The increased circulation and time to work off any tension you may be feeling will give you added energy.

PART IV

Exercises for Couples

9 · Exercising Together

Exercising with a companion can make a routine go a lot faster and be a lot of fun besides. This routine is designed for the use of two persons. Most of the movements will benefit both partners at the same time. Some of the movements allow one person to exercise while the other gives support or aid and at the same time gets a chance to catch his or her own breath.

Following this routine as it is set out will allow each person to get a fast-moving, effective physical-fitness workout. An ideal time to do this program is in the morning, before breakfast. This starts the circulation moving, warms stiff joints and limbers you both for a great beginning to your day.

Use your partner to keep the routine moving at a snappy pace. Don't allow yourself or your partner to lag. Keep yourself aware of your partner's movements as well as yours. We think you will find these exercises a great deal of fun, as we have, and very effective. If you find yourself away from a suitable place to train or if you are traveling and without access to weights, and you prefer resistance-type exercises, we think you will find these a good substitute for training with weights. Most important: Laugh and have a good time exercising together.

CHEST CROSSES

Purpose: This movement works the chest muscles and is most effective when each repetition is done slowly. Be sure to keep the elbows very slightly bent to place maximum effort on the chest muscles.

Equipment: None

Procedure: 1. Sit facing your partner. 2. Partner places hands inside your wrists. 3. Inhale and slowly move arms outward until they form a wide V with your upper body. 4. Slowly close arms together in front of you as your partner resists. Exhale.

Repetitions:

    Beginner 10 times

    Intermediate 15 times

    Advanced 20 times

TOWEL TRICEPS EXTENSION

Purpose: Both you and your partner will work the triceps muscles on this exercise. It should be done very slowly.

Equipment: A towel

Procedure: 1. Grasp both ends of towel behind neck while standing. Partner stands behind you and grasps middle of towel with both hands. 2. Inhale and slowly begin to straighten arms out as partner offers resistance. 3. When arms are almost straight, stop, resist, and exhale as your partner pulls downward. Both of you should inhale and exhale at the same times.

Repetitions:

> Beginner 10 times
> Intermediate 15 times
> Advanced 20 times

TOWEL CURL

Purpose: The person doing the curling movement is working biceps muscles while the partner resisting with the towel is working the latissimus dorsi and triceps muscles. For best results do this exercise very slowly.

Equipment: A towel

Procedure: 1. Stand grasping middle of towel with hands close together while partner holds onto ends of towel. 2. Inhale and curl the towel upward while partner resists. When hands reach chin slowly begin to lower hands as you exhale and partner resists on the way down. Both partners should inhale and exhale at the same times.

Repetitions:

    Beginner 10 times
    Intermediate 15 times
    Advanced 20 times

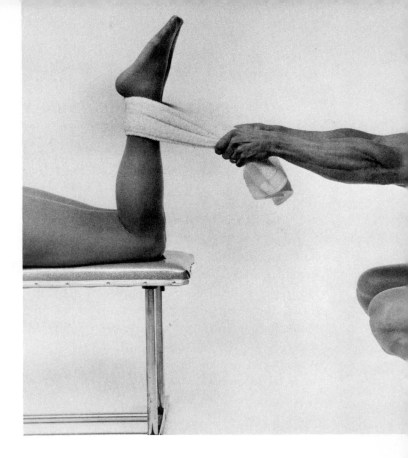

TOWEL LEG CURL

Purpose: This is a very good way to develop the leg biceps when you don't have access to a leg-curl machine. Resistance should be applied when raising and lowering legs, and the movement should be done slowly.

Equipment: A flat bench and a towel

Procedure: 1. Lie face down on a bench and hold onto sides with hands. Partner places towel around your ankles. 2. Inhale and slowly begin to curl the lower legs upward in an arc until heels almost touch buttocks. Partner resists by pulling on towel in the opposite direction. 3. Exhale and slowly lower legs to starting position as partner resists.

Repetitions:
> Beginner 10 times
> Intermediate 15 times
> Advanced 20 times

TWO-POSITION TOWEL NECK WORK

Purpose: To exercise the neck muscles and condition them to prevent stiff neck and headaches caused by sore neck muscles.

Equipment: Flat bench and towel

FIRST POSITION

Procedure: 1. Lie flat on back with head hanging off edge of bench. 2. Have partner place towel around forehead. 3. As partner pulls down on towel with both hands, inhale and resist slightly but allow head to bend downward. 4. When head reaches lowest position possible, force head slowly upward as you exhale. This works the frontal neck muscles.

SECOND POSITION

Procedure: 1. Lie flat on stomach with head hanging off the bench. 2. Have partner put towel around back of head. 3. As partner pulls down on towel with both hands, inhale and resist slightly but allow head to bend forward and downward. 4. When head reaches lowest position possible, force it slowly upward as you exhale. This works the rear neck muscles.

SEESAW

Purpose: With this exercise you and your partner will both be able to firm the waist, stomach and hips. Be sure to move as far forward and backward as possible. For a superstretch, keep your backs straight throughout the exercise.

Equipment: None

Procedure: 1. With a partner, sit on the floor and spread your legs wide. The partner with the more massive legs should place his or her feet on the inner calf of the other partner. This will brace you both as well as give you both an even balance. Take hold of your partner's hands. 2. Inhale as you lean backward while your partner exhales and comes forward. 3. Now alternate and you go forward, exhaling, as your partner leans backward, inhaling. 4. Be sure to do the movement as fully as possible. Keep your stomachs held in tight and firm.

Repetitions:
  Beginner 10 times
  Intermediate 15 times
  Advanced 20 times

CROSSOVER

Purpose: Both persons will be able to firm and trim waist and upper hips with this exercise as well as firm their legs. Get a good stretch and really reach out for maximum effectiveness.

Equipment: None

Procedure: 1. With your partner, sit on the floor with your legs spread as wide as possible. The person with the more massive legs should place his or her feet alongside ankles of partner. This will give you both equal balance in the movement. Grasp your partner's right hand with your right hand. 2. At the same time both of you swing your left hand to touch your right toes, exhaling as you reach. 3. Inhale as you sit back up, still holding right hands, and then repeat. 4. After you have completed your repetitions, change hands and work on the opposite side. 5. Breathe deeply and keep your stomachs held tight.

Repetitions:

Beginner 10 times

Intermediate 15 times

Advanced 20 times

CIRCLE-STRETCH

Purpose: Here you will be making a circular motion with your upper bodies as you both firm and trim your waistline, upper hips and midsection. Lean as far as possible from side to side.

Equipment: None

Procedure: 1. With your partner, sit on the floor facing each other with your legs spread. The person with the more massive legs should place his or her feet on the inside of the other's calves. This will give you both equal balance in the exercise. Hold on to your partner's hands. 2. You will be breathing in as you lean backward and out as you circle forward. 3. In a large circular motion, move clockwise for one full circle and counterclockwise another full circle. Continue alternating until all repetitions are completed.

Repetitions:
 Beginner 10 times
 Intermediate 15 times
 Advanced 20 times

SLIM-KICKS

Purpose: This is just about a total body exercise. Your partner and you will both be slimming and firming your waists, hips, buttocks, thighs and upper hip area. Be sure to keep your posture correct and both knees straight but not locked.

Equipment: None

Procedure: 1. Stand face to face with your partner, arms' distance apart. Grasp your partner's hands. Both of you should stand with feet slightly apart. 2. Hold your hands and body steady as you both swing your right legs toward your left, exhaling as you do so. 3. Inhale as you return your legs to the start position. 4. Now alternate and swing your left legs to the right side. 5. Be sure to lift the leg as high as is possible and point your toes.

Repetitions:

Beginner 10 times
Intermediate 15 times
Advanced 20 times

BENT-OVER TWISTS

Purpose: This is a fun exercise which will help loosen your trunk up as well as work on trimming that stubborn area on the upper hips. Both partners will benefit from this exercise at the same time. You will both notice your waists getting slimmer, too.

Equipment: None

Procedure: 1. Stand facing your partner, far enough apart so when you both bend forward at the waist your heads will be about 12 inches apart. Hold hands and bend over at the waist, extending your arms straight out to the sides. 2. Now you are ready for the exercise. Moving your upper body and arms only and keeping your arms straight, twist your body to the side, aiming one pair of hands toward the floor as the other pair is aimed toward the ceiling. Inhale as you twist to one side and exhale as you twist to the other side. 3. Alternate at a medium pace until you have completed all repetitions. 4. To really get a fabulous workout for the waist, hold your stomachs in tight. Remember not to move your feet or legs.

Repetitions:
> Beginner 10 times
> Intermediate 15 times
> Advanced 20 times

PARTIAL LIFT-UP

Purpose: One partner will be working his or her back muscles (the partner standing) and one partner will be working on firming and trimming hips, buttocks, and thighs (the partner doing the squatting movement). Both partners should hold their stomachs in tight and hold their legs tense for an added workout.

Equipment: None

Procedure: 1. Standing and facing your partner, grasp your hands on your partner's forearms near the elbows. Feet of both of you should be slightly apart, and the lighter partner may stand partly on the other's toes. 2. One partner will slowly bend his knees, leaning slightly back, and keeping his back straight as he lowers until his thighs are almost parallel to the floor, inhaling as he does so. The other person should lean slightly backward and keep his legs straight. This person will exhale as he bends forward. 3. Next, the partner who is in the squat position should begin exhaling and rise to the standing position as the standing person inhales and stands straight. 4. Now alternate roles and continue to do so until all repetitions are complete.

Repetitions:
    Beginner 10 times
    Intermediate 15 times
    Advanced 20 times

THIGH STRETCH

Purpose: This movement is excellent for strengthening a weak lower back while firming and loosening up the rear of your thighs. Breathe very deeply during this movement.

Equipment: None

Procedure: 1. Sit on the floor facing your partner. Both of you should have the left knee bent, with the sole of the left foot resting on the inside of the right leg. Grasp hands. 2. As you lean backward, pull your partner forward and inhale. Now let your partner pull you forward and exhale as you come forward as far as possible. Try to keep your back flat and pull forward, aiming to touch your chin to your knees. You may not be able to reach this far the first few times, but move slowly and, with a lot of practice, you both will make it eventually. 3. Now change legs and do all repetitions on the other side, working the left leg.

Repetitions:

    Beginner 10 times

    Intermediate 15 times

    Advanced 20 times

INNER THIGH SPREAD

Purpose: Here is an excellent exercise to firm the inner and outer thighs. Both partners will benefit from this exercise. When your legs are on the inside position you will be working the outer thigh. When your feet are on the outside position you will be working on the inner thigh.

Equipment: None

Procedure: 1. Lie on the floor facing your partner. Place your hands under your hips for support. Raise your legs high, one partner placing his feet on the inner ankles of the other. Hold them in this position. 2. Now the person with the outer position will push and resist the pressure of the partner with the inner position. Continue spreading and resisting with the ankles until the legs are open wide. Inhale while doing this. 3. Now begin exhaling as you close the legs, both partners resisting as they do so. 4. Continue the exercise until all repetitions are complete. Keep a constant tension on your legs at all times.

Repetitions:
Beginner 10 times
Intermediate 15 times
Advanced 20 times

BICYCLE PUSH

Purpose: This movement will work both partners' hips, thighs and buttocks. This exercise should be done at a moderate to fast pace.

Equipment: None

Procedure: 1. Sit on the floor facing your partner. Lean back on your hands for support. Bring your right knee up to your chest and extend your left leg. Place the soles of your feet on the soles of your partner's feet. 2. Now press and resist as you both move your feet in a cycling motion. Exhale as you extend the right leg and inhale as you extend the left.

Repetitions:
   Beginner 10 times
   Intermediate 15 times
   Advanced 20 times

RUNNING TOGETHER

Running is an activity that couples can do together. It is great for the heart, lungs and circulatory system and good for the muscles as well, especially the legs and hips.

If you haven't run regularly in a while, start with a quarter of a mile at a relaxing pace: say, take three minutes to complete the distance. We prefer running right after our workouts. A combination of running and weight training is probably one of the most effective fitness programs there is because it combines cardiovascular work with muscle developing.

If you can run six days a week you'll get great endurance after two or three weeks. As you get into better condition for running increase the distance to a mile and a half. If you can run this three times a week, that's fine. If you can do it six times a week, that's even better. We find that running a mile and a half at least three times a week works well in combination with bodybuilding exercises. Running helps to decrease the thickness of the layer of fat between the skin and the muscles; this decrease is noticeable after only a few weeks of conscientious running. After you are running your desired distance you can progress by trying to better your time on each occasion you run.

PART V

Competitive Bodybuilding

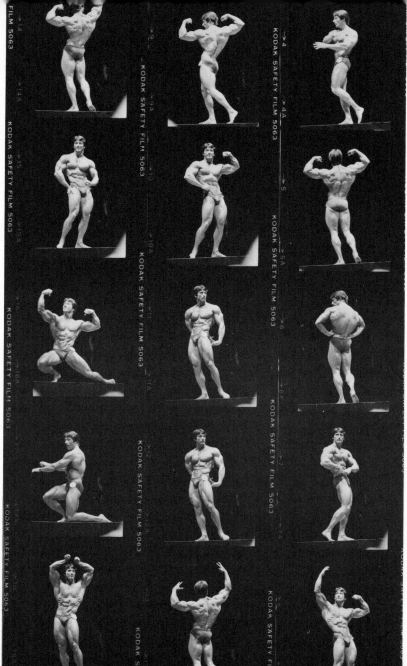

PHOTO CHRISTINE ZANE

190

10 · *What's It All About?*

After I had been training with weights I discovered there was such a thing as physique competition or competitive bodybuilding. It seemed to me to be somewhat like an art exhibition. In fact, I've always felt that the process of bodybuilding was analogous to sculpture. Yes, but living sculpture—creating the ideal body with scientific weight training principles. The idea appealed to me. And what better motivation to get into shape! A physique contest!

Well, I know a lot more about physique competition now than I did when I entered my first competition in 1961 at age eighteen. For one thing my body has become much more developed. This, however, could not have happened without knowing the complexities of advanced bodybuilding, which I will explain in this chapter.

Competitive bodybuilding can be divided into three categories: *Training* (which includes mental preparation, all weight, free form, and isometric exercises and running done in a bodybuilder's routine); *Nutrition* (including scientific use of the high protein low carbohydrate diet and vitamins, mineral and protein supplements); and *Posing,* in which a series of body positions or poses are arranged one after another to display the developed body to its fullest advantage.

In this section I will outline a training routine for the competitive bodybuilder. The exercises that appear in this section are done in a health studio or well-equipped home gym because they require special apparatus. These exercises are combined with the men's exercises in other parts of the book to make up the competitive bodybuilder's routine.

The Importance of Training Your Attention

The progress you make in bodybuilding is closely related to your ability to pay attention to exactly what you're doing during a workout. The stronger your attention, the deeper and more intense the workout. Have a 20-minute period where you center your attention on your breathing. This period should be immediately after you've eaten a small, easily digestible snack, as it will help digestion to proceed efficiently. Sit in a comfortable chair with spine erect, feet apart, hands on thighs, and close your eyes, breathe through your nose and relax. Just breathe normally—not too fast or too slow. Now, as you exhale, mentally count each breath, starting with one and proceeding through to ten. Every time your mind wanders, bring your attention back to the counting. If you lose count or count past ten start at one again. Continue doing this for at least 20 minutes. Then, as you finish, slowly open your eyes and continue to count breaths for another minute. Sit there for another few seconds and then slowly get up and gently shake your whole body. You should be in the gym ready to train within half an hour.

As you continue with these attention-training sessions before workouts, you will begin to notice several things. Your mind will become calm and clear, and this attitude will carry over into your workout period. As you practice training your attention, you will get to the point where you are not annoyed by distractions. The procedure when training in the gym is the same as when centering your attention. When distractions come up, you merely watch them briefly and then you return to what you were doing. You don't pursue or encourage the distraction. For example, if someone keeps interrupting your workouts, tell him "I can't answer your questions now because I'm concentrating on my workout. But I'd be glad to talk to you after I'm finished." Then return to your workout. Matters like these, once acknowledged, usually disappear.

THE COMPETITIVE BODYBUILDER'S PROGRAM

The competitive bodybuilder should train six days a week and rest on Sundays. Each body part is worked twice a week with the exception of calves, which are worked four times a week and abs which are worked every training day. This program can be done most of the year even when you are not training for a contest. You don't get bored with it because you're doing something different every day in three-day cycles. During this stage concentrate on using heavier weights than you have previously used in all your exercises. This will develop muscle thickness.

In my training, I stay at the beginning level for the first month of my training after a layoff, or period of no training. (I usually take a two-to-three-week layoff every year around the Christmas holidays.) After the initial soreness subsides and I start getting into better shape, I move on to the intermediate level. I stay at this level for three to five months and concentrate on increasing my exercise poundages. Then I move on to the advanced competitive routine which employs the double split routine, for the last two to three months of my training prior to a competition.

MONDAY AND THURSDAY:
SHOULDERS, CHEST, TRICEPS, ABDOMINALS

	BEGINNER			INTERMEDIATE		
EXERCISE/PAGE	sets	reps	weight	sets	reps	weight
Attention Training						
SHOULDERS						
Dumbbell Press 79	3	10	60	4	10	70
Upright Rowing 54	3	10	75	4	10	90
Alternate Dumbbell Front Raise 196	3	10	30	4	10	35
Side Raise 81	3	10	30	4	10	35
Incline Rear Dumbbell Raise 219	3	10	25	4	10	30
CHEST						
Bench Press 53	3	10	185	4	10	220
Incline Press 83	3	10	135	4	10	170
Dumbbell Flys 84	3	10	40	4	10	50
Dumbbell Pullover 56	3	10	60	4	10	70
Parallel Dips 197	3	10	0	4	10	0
TRICEPS						
Close Grip Bench Press 85	3	10	135	4	10	170

MONDAY AND THURSDAY:
SHOULDERS, CHEST, TRICEPS, ABDOMINALS (*cont.*)

	BEGINNER			INTERMEDIATE		
	sets	reps	weight	sets	reps	weight
Lying Extension 86	3	10	80	4	10	100
One-arm Dumbbell Extension 87	3	10	25	4	10	35
Dumbbell Kickback 198	3	10	20	4	10	30
ABDOMINALS						
Sit-up Over Bench 77	3	20	0	4	25	0
Leg Raise 47	3	20	0	4	25	0
Hanging Knee Up 199	3	15	0	4	20	0
Seated Twist 63	3	20	0	4	25	0
Hyperextension 200	1	20	0	2	25	0
Relaxation						

TUESDAY AND FRIDAY:
CALVES, BACK, BICEPS, FOREARMS, ABDOMINALS

	BEGINNER			INTERMEDIATE		
	sets	reps	weight	sets	reps	weight
CALVES						
Calf Machine Raises 201	3	15	180	4	20	220
Seated Calf Raise 202	3	15	100	4	20	150
BACK						
Wide Grip—Front Chin 68	3	10	0	4	12	0
Barbell—Bent-over Rowing 52	3	10	100–140	4	10	120–170
Dumbbell Rowing 70	3	10	70	4	10	85
Pulldown Behind Neck 203	3	10	150	4	10	170
BICEPS						
Concentration Curl 72	3	10	30	4	10	35
Alternate Dumbbell Curl 71	3	8	40	4	8	50
Incline Curl 204	3	10	30	4	10	40
Preacher Bench Curl 205	3	10	60	4	10	75
FOREARMS						
Reverse Curl 59	3	10	70	4	10	80
Wrist Curl 206	3	15	90	4	20	100
ABDOMINALS						
Sit-up Over Bench 77	3	20	0	4	25	0
Leg Raise 47	3	20	0	4	25	0
Hanging Knee Up 199	3	15	0	4	20	0
Seated Twist 63	3	20	0	4	25	0
Hyperextension 200	1	20	0	2	25	0
Relaxation						

WEDNESDAY AND SATURDAY:
THIGHS, CALVES, ABDOMINALS

	BEGINNER			INTERMEDIATE		
	sets	reps	weight	sets	reps	weight
THIGHS						
Leg Extension 207	3	15	50	4	20	70
Leg Press 208	3	10	150	4	10	200
Squat 72	3	10	135–185	4	10	135–225
Leg Curl 209	3	10	50	4	10	70
CALVES						
Calf Machine Raises 201	4	15	200	5	20	220
Seated Calf Raise 202	4	15	120	5	20	140
Donkeys 62	4	15	*	5	20	*
ABDOMINALS						
Sit-up Over Bench 77	3	20	0	4	25	0
Leg Raise 47	3	20	0	4	25	0
Hanging Knee Up 199	3	15	0	4	20	0
Seated Twist 63	3	20	0	4	25	0
Hyperextension 200	1	20	0	2	25	0
Relaxation						

*Partner Weight

PHOTO CHRISTINE ZANE

ALTERNATE DUMBBELL FRONT RAISE

Purpose: The front raise works the frontal deltoids. The secret of this exercise is to develop a rhythm as you raise and lower the dumbbells alternately.

Equipment: Two dumbbells

Procedure: 1. Start with a dumbbell held in each hand in front of you. 2. Inhale and raise one arm until dumbbell is above eye level. 3. Exhale as you lower dumbbell to starting position. 4. Repeat with other arm. This constitutes one repetition.

PARALLEL DIPS

Purpose: Depending on how you do them, parallel dips can work the lower pectorals, front deltoids, triceps and trapezius. I do parallel dips as chest work and I do them with no weight, stretching very low at the beginning of the movement and not coming all the way up at the end of the movement. I do dips using fast repetitions.

Equipment: A parallel dipping apparatus

Procedure: 1. Get up on the parallel bars grasping them with each hand. 2. Inhale and descend as low as possible, slowly at first. 3. When you reach bottom start ascending, using the force of the chest, shoulder, trapezius and tricep muscles. Exhale. Don't lock the elbows at the conclusion of the repetition because this takes tension off the pecs. Do each repetition more quickly than the previous one.

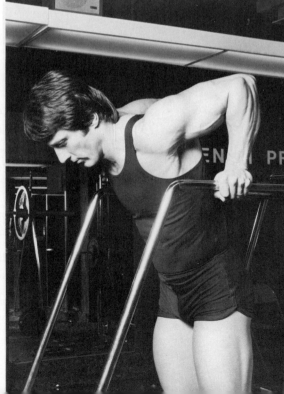

DUMBBELL KICKBACK

Purpose: Dumbbell kickback is best done face down on a 45-degree-incline bench. It is great for defining and bringing out the horseshoe shape to the triceps.

Equipment: Incline bench and two dumbbells

Procedure: 1. Lie face down on incline bench holding a dumbbell in each hand. Let your arms hang down to the side. Inhale, and 2. Bring dumbbells forward, bending arms at elbows. 3. Extend dumbbells back until arms are straight and hold for a count of two. Exhale and return to starting position.

HANGING KNEE UP

Purpose: Hanging knee up really works the lower abdominals. However, you must have a good grip in order to hang on to the bar. It is a good stretching movement—an excellent way to stretch and strengthen the lower back.

Equipment: Overhead bar

Procedure: 1. Grasp overhead bar with hands about one foot apart (feet should clear floor). Inhale, and 2. Pull knees upward until thighs touch stomach. Exhale. 3. Lower knees slowly until body is straight. By controlling pressure with your grip you can prevent swinging to and fro.

HYPEREXTENSION: SPINAL ERECTORS
(LOWER BACK)

Purpose: This exercise is one of the most effective ways to strengthen the lower back. I always do at least one set of 20 to 30 repetitions at the end of every workout. It's great for firming and developing the lower back.

Equipment: A hyperextension bench or other high bench with a means of holding the feet down (a leg curl table and a partner are perfect).

Procedure: 1. Lie face down over the edge of a high bench so that the bench makes contact with the lower abdomen. Fold arms across chest and lower upper body to floor. Inhale, and 2. Raise the upper body until it is parallel to the floor. 3. Exhale as you return to starting position.

CALF MACHINE RAISES

Purpose: Calf raises on a standing calf machine are a good all-around calf developer. Be sure to get a full range of movement with each repetition.

Equipment: Standing calf machine

Procedure: 1. Get in position under calf machine, positioning toes on a calf block. 2. Inhale and rise on toes as far as possible. 3. Exhale and descend as low as you can, doing this part of the movement slowly.

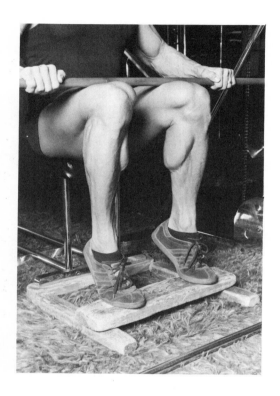

SEATED CALF RAISE

Purpose: This exercise can be used to widen the calf when viewed from the front if it is done in the regular manner because it works the soleus muscle. When the heels are turned outward the outer part of the gastrocnemius is worked.

Equipment: A seated calf machine

Procedure: 1. Sit on seated calf machine and put knees under pad. 2. Inhale and rise on toes as high as possible. 3. Lower the weight slowly all the way to bottom and exhale.

PULLDOWN

Purpose: Pulldowns and chins are similar movements, front pulldown and front chin being about the same and pulldown behind neck and chin behind neck being similar. So if you're doing front pull-downs, don't do front chin, etc. An advantage to pulldowns is that the weight is adjustable and the bar can usually be lowered further and a fuller range of motion is possible than in chins.

Equipment: Lat machine and someone to hold you down by pressing on your shoulders if the lat machine doesn't have an anchoring system.

Procedure: 1. Grasp bar with wide grip slightly wider than shoulder width. 2. Inhale and pull bar down until it touches top of chest, or until it touches behind neck. 3. Exhale and slowly let bar return to starting position. 4. Keep upper body straight throughout the movement.

INCLINE CURL

Purpose: Incline curls with dumbbells are very good for working the upper part of the biceps near the deltoid tie-in, and also the entire outer portion of the biceps. The lower the incline the more the upper biceps are worked (thus a 30-degree incline bench will more strongly affect this area than a 60-degree incline). It is important to keep the elbows anchored to the sides while doing this movement.

Equipment: Incline bench and a pair of dumbbells

Procedure: 1. Lie on an incline bench, grasp a pair of dumbbells in your hands, inhale. 2. Slowly curl the dumbbells upward while keeping the elbows at the sides (keep wrists straight). Stop when dumbbells touch shoulders. Exhale. Flex the biceps hard at the finish of the movement and slowly lower the dumbbells to starting position.

PREACHER BENCH CURL

Purpose: Preacher curls build the lower part of the biceps. The angle of the bench, the stationary position held when curling, and how the bar is held determine how well the biceps will be worked. The movement should be done slowly with not too heavy a weight. It is important to keep the wrists straight when curling and not relax the biceps and let the weight fall in at the top of the movement.

Equipment: A preacher bench and a barbell

Procedure: 1. Grasp a barbell with hands 12 inches apart and facing away from the body. Curl barbell up to chin. 2. Position arms 12 inches apart on preacher bench and, with wrists kept straight, lower the barbell until the arms are fully extended. Inhale. 3. Keeping wrists straight, curl the barbell upward until it is almost touching the chin. Exhale.

WRIST CURL

Purpose: This is the best exercise for developing the bottom part of the forearm muscles. Not too heavy a weight should be used, as high repetitions are necessary. Wrist curl is also very good for strengthening the grip.

Equipment: Barbell and a bench to sit on

Procedure: 1. Sit on the end of a bench, bend forward at the waist, grasp a barbell with palms facing up, positioning hands about 12 inches apart. 2. Rest forearms on thighs so that barbell hangs over knees. 3. Inhale and rotate barbell upward as far as possible. 4. Pause briefly and exhale as you slowly lower barbell to starting position.

LEG EXTENSION

Purpose: Leg extension is the best movement for defining the muscles of the frontal thigh when done with high repetitions. It also strengthens the muscles above the knees and is often used by people with knee injuries. Each repetition should be done slowly, keeping constant tension on the frontal thigh muscles.

Equipment: A leg extension table

Procedure: 1. Sit on a leg extension table and put feet behind lower pad. Hold on to the side of table with hands. 2. Inhale and raise apparatus until legs are parallel with floor. 3. Exhale as you slowly lower to starting position.

LEG PRESS

Purpose: Leg press is a good overall thigh exercise, and it is especially effective for the lateral part of the thigh. Hips should always be a few inches higher than the shoulders when doing leg press. Also toes should make contact with leg press board.

Equipment: Leg press machine

Procedure: 1. Lie under leg press machine so that your hips are exactly under the machine. Put feet on leg press board, making contact with toes and ball of foot. 2. Remove supports, inhale, and lower weight slowly. 3. When weight is in correct position press it upward with the force of the thigh muscles. Exhale. Don't lock the knees at the end of each repetition.

LEG CURL

Purpose: Leg curl is the best way to develop the leg biceps. When doing the movement try not to let the hips come up off the table, as this takes tension off the leg biceps and puts more of it on the buttocks.

Equipment: A leg curl table

Procedure: 1. Lie face down on leg curl table with ankles behind pad. 2. Inhale and slowly curl the apparatus upward as far as possible. 3. Exhale as you slowly return the apparatus to starting position.

PROGRAM FOR THE ADVANCED
COMPETITIVE BODYBUILDER

This program is to be followed the two to three months before a competition as your time schedule permits. It is an all-out training program, and you'll need extra rest. It is a good idea to arrange to get a one-hour nap during the day in addition to the eight hours of sleep you get at night. The program goes this way: Monday, Wednesday, Friday mornings you train back, biceps, forearms and abs; Monday, Wednesday, Friday afternoons you train thighs, calves and abs. Tuesday, Thursday, Saturday mornings (or afternoons) you train shoulders, chest, triceps and abs. You can also do a calf workout on one of these days if you feel your calves need more improvement. So, in effect, you are getting nine workouts a week. Very rapid improvement can be made on this program but it takes a lot of energy.

The purpose of such an intensive workout schedule is to develop a maximum amount of muscularity. Muscularity can be described as a combination of size, definition and separation. Size refers to how big the muscle is. Definition means the degree of striation the muscle shows, and separation is how well each muscle group stands apart from the others. In other words, definition is development within a muscle and separation is development between muscles. Intensive training done the last few months before a competition will increase size, definition and separation when combined with proper rest and nutrition.

MONDAY, WEDNESDAY, FRIDAY MORNINGS:
BACK, BICEPS, FOREARMS, ABDOMINALS

EXERCISE/PAGE	*sets*	*reps*	*weights**
Attention Training			
BACK			
Front Chin 68	5	12	
Bent-over Rowing 52	5	10	100, 120, 140, 160, 180
Dumbbell Rowing 70	4	10	75
Pulldown Behind Neck 203	4	10	180
One-arm Cable Row: Nonstop Sets 213	3	10	50
BICEPS			
Dumbbell Concentration Curl 72	4	10, 8, 7, 6	30, 35, 40, 45
Alternate Dumbbell Curl 71	4	10, 8, 7, 6	40, 45, 50, 55

MONDAY, WEDNESDAY, FRIDAY MORNINGS:
BACK, BICEPS, FOREARMS, ABDOMINALS *(cont.)*

EXERCISE/PAGE	*sets*	*reps*	*weights**
Attention Training			
Incline Curl 204	4	10	35
Barbell Curl 57	4	10	100
Preacher Bench Curl 205	4	10	70
FOREARMS			
Reverse Curl 59	5	10	70, 80, 90, 90, 90
Wrist Curl 206	5	15	90, 100, 110, 110, 110
Reverse Wrist Curl 214	5	15	30
ABDOMINALS			
Hanging Knee Up 199	4	25	
Incline Knee-in 78	4	25	
Partial Sit-up 215	4	25	
Hyperextension 200	1	25	
Relaxation			

* These multiple listings under weights mean that you should increase your poundages on every set.

MONDAY, WEDNESDAY, FRIDAY AFTERNOONS:
THIGHS, CALVES, ABDOMINALS

EXERCISE/PAGE	*sets*	*reps*	*weights*
Attention Training			
THIGHS			
Leg Extension 207	4	25, 20, 15, 10	50, 60, 70, 80
Leg Press 208	4	10	150, 175, 200, 225
Squat 72	4	10	135, 185, 225, 245
Hack Squat 74	4	10	25-lb. Dumbbells
Leg Curl 209	4	10	60
CALVES			
Calf Machine Raises 201	5	15	300
Seated Calf Raise 202	5	15	125
Donkeys 62	5	20–25	Partner (same body weight as you)
Leg Press Calf Raise 216	3	15	200
One-legged Calf Raise 76	3	15	0
ABDOMINALS			
Sit-up Over Bench 77	4	25	
Leg Raise 47	4	25	
Seated Twist 63	1	100	
Hyperextension 200	1	25	
Relaxation			

TUESDAY, THURSDAY, SATURDAY MORNINGS:*
CHEST, SHOULDERS, TRICEPS, ABDOMINALS
(Calves on Saturday only)

EXERCISE/PAGE	sets	reps	weights
Attention Training			
CHEST			
Bench Press 53	5	15, 12, 10, 8, 6	135, 185, 225, 245, 265
Incline Press 83	4	10, 8, 7, 6	155, 175, 195, 195
Dumbbell Flys 84	4	10	45
Dumbbell Pullover 56	4	10	75
Superset { Cable Crossovers 217	4	15	20
{ Parallel Dips 197	4	10	0
SHOULDERS			
Dumbbell Press 79	4	10, 8, 7, 6	60, 65, 70, 75
Alternate Dumbbell Front Raise 196	4	10	25–30
One-dumbbell Front Raise 221	4	10	50+
Side Raise 81	4	0	30–40
Side Cable Raise 218	4	10	10
Incline Rear Dumbbell Raise 219	4	10	25–30
Dumbbell Rear Raise 82	4	10	25–30
TRICEPS			
Close Grip Bench Press 85	4	10	135–175
Lying Triceps Extension 86	4	10	80–100
One-arm Dumbbell Extension 87	4	10	30
Dumbbell Kickback 198	4	10	25
Reverse Dips 42	4	10	0
ABDOMINALS			
Sit-up Over Bench 77	4	25	0
Leg Raise 47	4	25	0
Incline Knee-in 78	4	25	0
Seated Twist 63	1	100	0
Hyperextension 200	2	25	0
Relaxation			

* This routine can be divided into two separate workouts: Tuesday, Thursday, Saturday mornings—chest, triceps, and abdominals; Tuesday, Thursday, Saturday afternoons—deltoids, abdominals. Calves—Tuesday and/or Saturday. This would give two daily workouts six days a week for a total of 12 workouts each week.

ONE-ARM CABLE ROW

Purpose: A good exercise to stretch and develop the lower part of the latissimus dorsi muscle on each side. It's important to let the arm extend fully and slowly to get a maximum stretch with each rep.

Equipment: A low pulley

Procedure: 1. Stand sideways to low pulley with feet about 24 inches apart. Grab handle of pulley with hand farthest away from pulley. Bend forward at waist with knees slightly bent and other hand resting on knee. 2. Inhale and pull handle until it touches chest. 3. Exhale as you slowly let handle return to starting position, stretching the lower latissimus muscle by leaning forward slightly in the direction of the pulley. 4. Switch hands and assume opposite body position after doing a set with one hand.

213

REVERSE WRIST CURL

Purpose: This exercise should be done with a very light weight for high repetitions. It works the top part of the forearm. The movement should be done slowly with a full range of motion.

Equipment: Flat bench and light barbell

Procedure: 1. Sit on bench and grasp barbell with a reverse grip and hands about six inches apart. 2. Bring wrists over knees with palms facing downward, bending slightly forward with the upper body. 3. Inhale and raise the weight up toward the body. Pause. 4. Exhale as you lower the weight slowly, letting the bar descend downward as far as possible. 5. Inhale as you bring the bar upward for the second repetition.

PARTIAL SIT-UP

Purpose: Partial sit-up is a very good exercise for the rectus abdominals because it works them directly. Its secret is in thrusting the hips and raising the head and shoulders at exactly the same time. Twist your head and shoulders to one side and you'll work the intercostal muscles. This exercise works the upper portion of the rectus (frontal) abdominals.

Equipment: Something to put your feet on three feet above where you're lying

Procedure: 1. Lie flat on back with feet elevated three feet and knees bent. Inhale. 2. Thrust hips upward and lift head and shoulders off floor (or bench). Exhale. 3. Do this movement slowly.

CALF RAISE ON LEG PRESS MACHINE

Purpose: This is a very good exercise to develop the calves, especially the lower part. It works the lower part because gravity forces the weight downward at the start of each repetition.

Equipment: Leg press machine

Procedure: 1. Lie under leg press machine in same position as in Leg Press (page 208). 2. Keeping knees slightly unlocked, inhale and raise weight upward (toes make contact with leg press board) with force of calf muscles. 3. Exhale and lower weight as far as it will go. Be sure to get a good stretch at the bottom.

CABLE CROSSOVERS

Purpose: This exercise works both the outer and the inner portion of the pectorals. Get a good stretch at the start where the arms are fully extended for the outer pecs and a hard concentration as you cross the cable handles in front of you for the inner pecs.

Equipment: A double-handle pulley apparatus

Procedure: 1. Grasp a cable handle in each hand, extend arms outward at sides, spread feet about 24 inches apart. 2. Bend slightly forward, inhale and bring the cable handles toward each other using the strength of the pectoral muscles. Continue this until the handles have crossed each other. Exhale.

217

SIDE CABLE RAISE

Purpose: This movement specifically works the lateral and rear deltoid junction. It should be done with arm straight, slowly, with not too much weight on the pulley.

Equipment: A pulley system

Procedure: 1. Grasp cable handle in one hand, put other hand on hip and stand sideways from the pulley system. 2. Inhale and raise handle sideways (slightly backward) turning the wrist outward as you raise the handle to shoulder level. 3. Slowly lower the handle to starting position. Exhale.

218

INCLINE REAR DUMBBELL RAISE

Purpose: This is my favorite exercise for rear deltoids. It is important to raise the dumbbells slightly forward and to turn the wrists outward as you raise the dumbbells upward.

Equipment: 45-degree incline bench and a pair of dumbbells

Procedure: 1. Lie face down on an incline bench, holding a moderately weighted dumbbell in each hand. 2. Inhale and raise the dumbbells sideways, twisting the wrists outward as you raise them. The dumbbells should be raised slightly forward. 3. Lower the dumbbells slowly to starting position. Exhale.

SERRATUS LEVERS ON PULLDOWN MACHINE

Purpose: This exercise develops the serratus when done with elbows slightly bent and upper body leaning slightly forward. A relatively light weight should be used here and you should get a rhythm to all repetitions. You should also feel this movement working the rear section of the triceps.

Equipment: A lat machine

Procedure: 1. Lean forward at waist. With arms extended above head and in front of you with elbows slightly bent, and with a close grip, grasp lat bar. 2. Inhale and force bar downward in an arc until it touches thighs. 3. Exhale as you slowly allow the bar to return to starting position. Do not rest by allowing tension on the serratus muscles to ease up during any part of this movement.

ONE-DUMBBELL FRONT RAISE

Purpose: This exercise works the frontal deltoids. It is good because constant tension is kept on the front delts as the weight is raised and lowered.

Equipment: One dumbbell

Procedure: 1. Grasp the dumbbell in the middle with both hands, fingers interlaced. 2. Inhale and raise the dumbbell to eye level. 3. Slowly lower the dumbbell to starting position. Exhale.

11 · Essentials of Competitive Bodybuilding

THE WORKOUT JOURNAL

I find it useful to keep a written record of my workouts. After each workout I write out all of my exercises, the weights I used and how many reps I did with each weight. I also write down how I felt during the workout: did I get a good pump, did I lack energy, did I sustain an injury, was I distracted, etc. I prefer doing this at home following the training session, rather than between sets at the gym, because the latter way would interrupt the flow of my workout. The journal is useful because I can see exactly what I've done on paper and I can measure my progress this way. The journal should be reviewed every week to give you a good idea of how you are doing and what you plan to do. Resolve to do better!

TRAINING PARTNER

Training with a partner has several advantages. Your training becomes easier because you have someone to push you in your workout. It also makes training more interesting because competition is involved. Whenever I'm in training for a competition, I always try to find a training partner because I know I'll train harder.

When choosing a training partner, pick one who has a similar structure to yours and similar weak points. Agree upon the training program and the time of day, and how often you will train beforehand. Encourage each other while you train and reward each other with praise when you surpass former training records. Whenever one of you is distracted from the workout by talking to someone else, he should be reminded by the other partner that it's time to do his next set. You should watch each other as you do your sets and get into the habit of resting only as long between sets as it takes your partner to finish his set. You'll get a lot of work done in a shorter period of time this way and you'll get a better pump and a more intensive workout.

SPECIALIZATION PROGRAMS

You will probably find that certain parts of your body improve faster than other parts. The way to get around this is by (A) working your weak points first in your workout when your energy, strength and attention are greatest; (B) doing more sets with heavier weights* for areas lagging in development; (C) working the unresponsive body parts two days in succession, resting this area on the third day, and then training it again two more days in succession. If I am using specialization on some body part and training it several days in succession, I usually train this area with different exercises each day. For example, if I'm working shoulders, I might do press behind neck, upright rowing and bent-over lateral raise the first day, and dumbbell press, side dumbbell raise and rear incline raise the following day. This method can be used with any body part but shouldn't be continued for longer than one month. After a month you should be able to make the progress you desire. I often use this method when training for an exhibition or competition and some body part isn't responding as I'd like it to.

FORCED REPS AND NEGATIVE RESISTANCE TRAINING

Building Size and Strength

Remember that there are two parts to every bodybuilding movement: 1. moving the weight from starting to finishing position; 2. moving the weight back from finish to starting position. You should be in control of the weight at all times. Many bodybuilders concentrate only on moving the weight from start to finish position, but the

* A heavy weight only allows the bodybuilder to do six to ten reps with it.

second half of the movement is equally important. This part from finish to starting position is called *negative resistance,* and by concentrating and moving the weight slowly back to starting position a great deal of muscle size and strength can be developed. Negative resistance is especially effective with barbell movements like bench press and barbell curl, but it can be utilized with all exercises.

Another way to build muscle size, strength and muscularity is by doing *forced reps.* This means to keep doing repetitions even after you can do no more with the weight you're using. This can be done by either of two ways: 1. By having someone lighten the resistance by placing his hands on the weight and helping you raise it; 2. By letting someone remove weight from the training apparatus after you've done as many reps as you can with the weight. A word of caution: Do several sets first and make sure the muscles are completely warmed up before doing forced reps. If you are not warmed up, you are inviting injury.

SUPERSETS AND TRI-SETS
Good When Training Alone

A superset is doing two different exercises one after the other, with little or no rest between each exercise. Tri-sets are the same idea, but with three exercises. Supersets and tri-sets are a good change of pace from regular sets; they give a good pump and help you move through your workout more quickly, especially if you are training alone. They are more successfully used to build muscular definition than to build size, because the amount of weight used is less than in single sets due to the fact that the muscles involved tire faster. Exercises for the same body part or adjacent body parts can be supersetted or tri-setted; just don't superset or tri-set similar exercises. This will reduce the efficiency of the exercises because you'll be forced to use very light weights to do the movements correctly.

ISOMETRICS, RUNNING, JUMPING ROPE

Isometric exercises, or resistance exercise without movement, are something you can do to increase strength and muscularity the last month or so before a competition. They should be done every day and only take a few minutes. The series of exercises for arms and shoulders (doorway and doorknob isometrics; see pages 43 and 44) are excellent for this purpose.

Running and *jumping rope* are excellent ways to develop endurance, reduce the amount of subcutaneous fat on the body, and develop the legs. I find it helpful to run one to two miles daily, or skip rope for five to ten minutes each day when I'm training for a competition. Jumping rope is very convenient because it can be done practically anywhere and it is very good for bringing out muscular definition in the calves. I usually jump rope for about one minute and then rest for one minute before I proceed to my next set.

OVERTRAINING

The secret of making gains in bodybuilding is to do just enough training to get results and no more. Doing more training than necessary can result in excessive soreness and overtraining. If you ever get overtrained, your energy level will drop, you'll feel very tired, your muscularity won't be as sharp, and you may lose a few pounds. When I'm feeling overtrained, I take a few days off from training and increase my carbohydrate intake slightly.

A QUICK MUSCLE-SIZE-BUILDING PROGRAM

If you find that you cannot gain muscle size, you may be overtraining. Take two to three days off from training by cutting down to three sets each of three to four different exercises per body part. This makes a total of 9 to 12 sets per body part. The smaller the muscle group, the fewer sets it needs to build size.

The first set is a warm-up set with a weight tthat permits 15 to 20 reps. Add weight so that only five to eight reps are possible on the third set. Rest only long enough between sets to allow breathing to return to normal. Work each body part twice a week this way. (Work calves three times a week. Abs are worked as before.) Use this routine as long as you make gains from it.

LAYOFFS

It has been my experience that if I train hard and reach a physical peak for a physique competition, then I must balance this period of very hard training with a complete rest, a period of inactivity or layoff. I like to take this break from training after my competitive season is over; this usually occurs during the month of December, around the Christmas holidays and the New Year. During this time I also eat whatever I feel like eating and forget about training completely. After about two or three weeks of this the desire to train starts to build up inside me again and I return to my training with much more enthusiasm than if I hadn't taken a layoff. My concept of training for competitive bodybuilding is that it is seasonal, just like training for any other sport such as football or baseball. The athletes who participate in these sports don't train all year round but their training involves a getting-in-shape phase that precedes the regular season; this is followed by a period of inactivity in their sport after the season is over. It is mentally healthy, too, to have a layoff, as this gives you a refreshing change of pace as well as giving your body a chance to recuperate from injuries incurred during the training season.

DIETING AND VITAMIN-MINERAL SUPPLEMENTS

The best way to reduce the amount of fat on the body, aside from regular training, is by following a low carbohydrate diet. I limit my carbohydrate to 20 grams a day* or less the last month before a competition. This way I use up fat stored in the body for energy purposes and I become more muscular.

I also supplement my diet with vitamins and minerals. Vitamins and minerals produce enzymes in the body. These enzymes control reactions vital to life. The following vitamins and minerals are most important:

Fat-soluble vitamins

Vitamin A–Improves skin texture and keeps linings of throat, nose and digestive tract healthy.

* Daily carbohydrate intake varies between individuals. Some people may need more.

Vitamin D–Helps normal growth of bones and teeth.

Vitamin E–Essential for the proper functioning of the heart and circulatory system and the reproductive system, and is an anti-oxidant.

Water-soluble vitamins

B complex–Keeps appetite and digestion normal, nervous system healthy, and helps prevent irritability and fatigue; also helps the body utilize protein and carbohydrates and fats for energy. There are 12 known vitamins of the B complex.

Vitamin C–Builds resistance to infection, helps healing of fractures and wounds and production of intercellular connective tissue, aids in strengthening capillaries, bones and gums, and assists in the proper utilization of iron. As an anti-oxidant it helps protect against pollution from the environment.

Bioflavonoids and rutin–Aid in the body's utilization of vitamin C.

Minerals and trace minerals

Calcium–Helps the development and maintenance of strong bones and teeth, assists normal blood clotting, muscle action, heart and nerve function.

Phosphorus–Works with calcium in nerve response to stimuli and muscle contraction.

Iron–Combines with protein to form hemoglobin, which carries oxygen to the cells.

Iodine–Helps regulate mental and physical development and general metabolism as a component of the hormone thyroxin.

Magnesium–Aids in reduction of blood pressure, relaxation of nerves and construction of body protein.

Chlorine, copper, fluorine, manganese, potassium, sodium, vanadium and zinc are important factors in maintaining physiological processes and act as aids in digestion, proper bone and tooth formation, proper functioning of the nervous system, heart, muscles, kidneys and enzyme systems, and regulation of body fluids. The efficiency of each mineral is enhanced by the right amounts of other nutrients. Vitamins cannot function in the absence of certain minerals.

WARMING UP AND INJURIES

It is very important to keep warm while training, especially if you are handling heavy weights. If the weather is warm, you need only wear comfortable training clothing. But if it's cold, you'll need warmer training gear. Always warm up on each exercise before you start using heavier weights. This can be done by stretching or bending movements or by doing high repetitions in the exercise itself, using a light weight.

Be careful to avoid injury by always keeping warm while exercising and warming up. However, if you should get an injury, a chiropractic adjustment and/or ultrasound or sinusoidal current applied to the injured area can help. Moist heat applied to injuries, as in a whirlpool bath, is often helpful. If an area is extremely sore, I often rub ice cubes on it for a few minutes for relief.

It's uncomfortable to train hard when you have a muscle injury. I found the best thing to do is to perform exercises that work the injured muscles but use very light weights and high repetitions. Thirty repetitions of two to three sets will bring a fresh blood supply into the injured area and can help healing to take place more quickly. As the injury heals, begin very gradually to increase the amount of weight used and decrease the repetitions.

TANNING

Nothing enhances the physique more than a deep, even tan. Lying in the sun will dehydrate you slightly, the more so in a dry climate. Gradually build up your tan over a two-month period. Use an oil containing PABA and/or lanolin, and rub on an aloe cream or gel after you shower. Don't use baby oil. Avocado oil is a very good skin softener and can be used if the skin is dry.

POSING

Posing, or displaying the muscles of the body on stage, can be called "kinetic sculpture." To me bodybuilding is very much like sculpture because I use weight-training apparatus and nutritional principles to create my body as I wish.

There are two distinct aspects of posing: tension and movement. Tension involves tensing all the muscles of the body (except the facial muscles) and holding the pose. This is the static aspect of posing. Movement involves moving gracefully and dynamically from one pose to the next. This is the kinetic aspect.

The following photos illustrate some of my favorite poses, which I combine in a sequence to form a posing routine performed to music.

"Posedown" to determine the final overall winner at the Mr. Olympia. Left to right: Robbie Robinson, Frank Zane, Dennis Tinnerino, and Ed Corney.

Frank Zane being congratulated after winning Mr. Olympia. Left to right:
Boyer Coe, Ed Corney, Frank Zane, Robbie Robinson, and
Dennis Tinnerino.

PHOTO CHRISTINE ZANE

Pages 235 through 239:
Individual posing presentations during the Mr. Olympia contest.

Joe Weider (left) and Ben Weider raising the winner's hands at the 1977
Mr. Olympia.

PHOTO CHRISTINE ZANE

PHOTO CHRISTINE ZANE

238

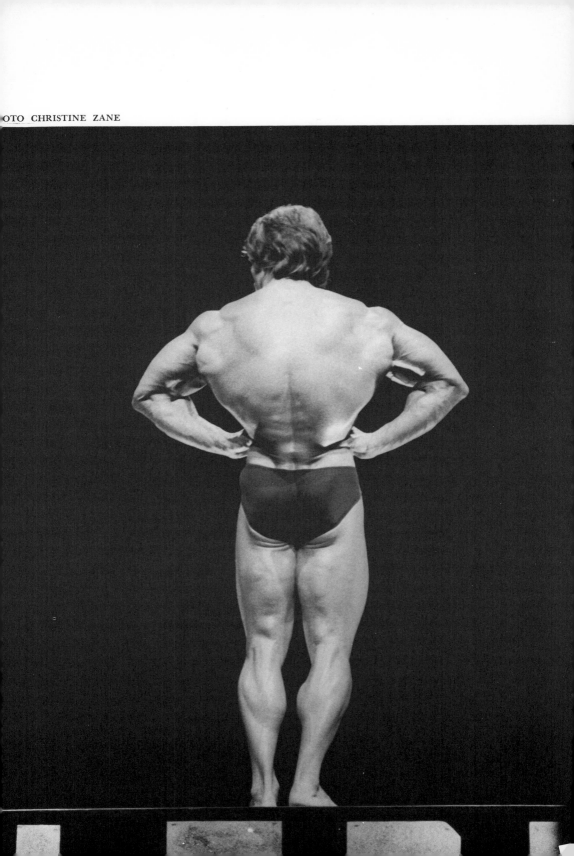

PHOTO KENN DUNCAN

240

PHOTO KENN DUNCAN

241

PHOTO RHEO BLAIR

PHOTO RHEO BLAIR

Appendix · Nutrition

We have traveled for much of our married life together giving physical-culture exhibitions and bodybuilding seminars and have become extremely interested in nutrition. We have found that as a couple it is simple to help each other stay in shape and eat the proper foods. For example, by not keeping junk foods around (like white sugar and white flour products) we are less prone to eat them. Our relationship has developed into one that emphasizes training, nutrition, and mutual concern for each other's physical welfare.

Nutrition plays a big part in both of our training programs. We have never spared any expense to eat the finest, freshest and most nutritious foods available. When you realize that the food you eat eventually becomes your body, you begin to understand how important nutrition really is. Your body is built from the food you eat. Just look at the bodies of those people who eat at hot dog and hamburger stands and you'll see that the majority of these people don't look so good. It's very important to eat correctly and select the most nutritious foods you can afford.

Begin by cleaning up your diet; remove the "junk foods," the empty calories. Eliminate refined sugar and products that contain sugar from your diet. Refined sugar gives you no vitamins or minerals and destroys certain nutrients in your body (calcium and B vitamins) essential for muscular growth. We use small amounts of glycerin instead, which can be purchased at any drug store. Glycerin is used more slowly by the body for energy purposes and one teaspoon is equal to one teaspoon of sugar in sweetening power. Junk foods like candies, cakes, pies, sodas are loaded with sugar and should be avoided. The problem with these refined sugar products is that they elevate the blood-sugar level too quickly, causing a rush of energy, only to be followed by a drastic drop of the blood-sugar level within an hour. This causes a nervous, weak, irritable feeling in the body. Coffee and alcohol also play havoc with the blood sugar. Fresh fruits are a better source of energy, and also contain varying amounts of vitamins and minerals. Eating small amounts of carbohydrates is important for keeping the blood-sugar level up. This gives energy, which is needed before any exercise can be done.

Good nutrition is important because it makes you healthy. Bodybuilding is much more productive if the person is healthy. Exercise actually tears down the muscle tissue. It's good nutrition and rest that build muscle cells. A combination of exercise, nutrition, adequate rest and positive mental attitudes is essential for bodybuilding progress.

CARBOHYDRATES

Sugars and starches are carbohydrates which are needed in the body for energy purposes, and these carbohydrates should include fruits and especially vegetables and whole grains. We have found that in order to keep the amount of fat on the body at a minimum, it is necessary to limit our daily consumption of carbohydrates to around 20 to 50 grams. Then every fourth or fifth day we increase this amount to around 60 to 80 grams. We've been doing this for the past several years with gratifying results.

Vegetables are good sources of energy, perhaps better than fruits, because energy released from vegetables is even more gradual so you feel better for a longer period of time. One fourth to one half of a baked potato, with the jacket left on and served with sour cream, is a tremendous energy food. Brown rice is also a very good energy food. Other vegetables like celery, lettuce, spinach, red and green peppers, cucumbers, mushrooms, onions, asparagus, zucchini, crookneck summer squash, alfalfa sprouts: all these are excellent low-carbohydrate vegetables, easily prepared by cooking quickly in a vegetable steamer—or they can be eaten raw.

Another good source of carbohydrate is whole-grain bread, which can be obtained in any health-food store. A small amount of whole-grain bread eaten with butter is a great energy source. Make sure the bread you buy contains no sugar, preservatives, softeners or bleached flour.

We eat only the low-carbohydrate fruits: cherries, strawberries, cantaloupes, honeydews, avocados (probably the best fruit for keeping the blood sugar up), tomatoes and occasionally grapefruit and apples.

PROTEINS

Protein is a very important nutrient for bodybuilding. When proteins are eaten they are broken down into amino acids in the stomach and absorbed into the body and used for growth and repair. For maintaining or losing body weight, one gram of protein should be consumed for each two to two and a half pounds of present body weight. Thus a 150-pound person would eat around 60 to 75 grams of protein daily. For gaining body weight, one gram of protein should be eaten for each pound of body weight. Thus a person weighing 150 pounds would eat approximately 150 grams of protein daily.

The best protein foods are those most easily utilized by the body. A protein is rated "assimilable" in accordance with how efficiently it is utilized by the body. Not all proteins are equally assimilable. The most assimilable protein foods are eggs, milk, and other dairy products. Meat, fish, and poultry are not as assimilable as dairy products and eggs. Vegetable proteins like soya and yeast are even less assimilable. We ourselves eat protein foods according to their assimilability. Eggs are high on our list, as they are a nearly perfect food. In regard to the cholesterol controversy, prominent nutritionists and biochemists agree that the cholesterol contained in eggs does not lead to high cholesterol levels in the body.* The culprit seems to be excessive intake of refined carbohydrates such as sweets. Hard and semisoft cheeses are excellent foods, as are cottage cheese, ricotta cheese, and

* R. Passwater. *Supernutrition for Healthy Hearts.* New York: Dial Press.

yogurt. Milk is also a good food but may cause an increase of the amount of fat on the body because it contains the sugar lactose.

Of the meats, lamb is one of our favorites. We also eat small amounts of beef and pork. Chicken, turkey and duck are excellent protein foods too, as are all varieties of fish. Organ meats like liver and heart are also nutritious and tasty when prepared properly. Anyone interested in building muscle should eat meats regularly. They give you strength and energy. Even if you're not interested in getting bigger muscles, you should eat meat a few times a week to keep your strength up. Of the vegetable proteins, we feel that yeast is the best one because it contains substantial amounts of B vitamins and amino acids. A protein powder is an excellent way to get more protein in your system. A protein drink made from milk and egg protein powder mixed with fresh whole or skimmed milk sipped slowly can provide as much nourishment as a large meal and can occasionally be substituted for one if you are in a hurry. Protein drinks or milk should never be gulped down because this can cause them to curdle in the stomach and cause an upset stomach or a sour feeling in the digestive tract.

FATS

Fats are the third main class of foods. Their primary function is to provide long-term energy (over a period of several hours). They prevent you from feeling hungry because they take longer to empty out of the stomach. Fats are also needed for healthy hair, skin, and certain body tissues. Fats are of two types: saturated—cream, butter, sour cream, fat from meats—and unsaturated—vegetable oils like corn oil, safflower oil, wheat-germ oil, olive oil, avocado oil. Your body needs both kinds of fat. Many people strictly avoid saturated fats because they think this will make them gain weight or fat on their bodies. There is evidence against this. However, too high an intake of unsaturated fats can destroy certain nutrients in your body like vitamin E.*

We mainly use the fats just mentioned and consume slightly more saturated fats than unsaturated fats.

* A. Hoffer. "Supernutrition," in *A Physician's Handbook on Orthomolecular Medicine*. New York: Pergamon Press.

Diets for Gaining Weight Gradually

Everyone who starts bodybuilding or free-form exercise usually wants either to gain weight or to lose weight.

If you want to gain weight it's better to eat small amounts of food frequently throughout the day than to eat three large meals. This keeps the waistline smaller and allows the food to be digested more efficiently. Here is a sample menu that Frank often uses when he wishes to gain weight gradually. It provides for five or six small meals instead of three large ones.

Breakfast: 7 A.M.

3 eggs, any style
bacon or ham (2 to 4 ounces)
½ slice whole-grain toast with butter
1 cup herb tea with 1 teaspoon glycerin

Snack: 10 A.M.

8 ounces whole milk (certified raw if available)
½ cup milk-egg protein powder
1 raw egg yolk
1 teaspoon glycerin
handful of fresh or frozen strawberries, without added sugar (optional)
    Blend all of the above well in a blender.

Lunch: 1 P.M.

7½ ounces tuna or salmon (water-packed or drain off oil)
mayonnaise: 1 to 2 tablespoons
tomatoes and/or alfalfa sprouts
1 hard-cooked egg
    Arrange all of the above attractively to make a salad.
8 ounces club soda

Snack: 4 P.M.

same as 10 A.M.
    or
cottage cheese or yogurt with strawberries, cantaloupe, or honeydew melon

Dinner: 7 P.M.
Small dinner salad with oil and vinegar (tomatoes, lettuce, avocado, mushrooms, sprouts, etc.)
generous portion of beef, pork, lamb, chicken, turkey, or broiled fish
2 ounces cheese
8 ounces club soda

This daily menu gives an ample amount of protein, some fat, and some carbohydrates. The mealtimes listed are approximate. According to this schedule the best time for exercising would be one hour after either of the snacks (i.e., 11 A.M. or 5 P.M.), or two hours after each main meal (i.e., 9 A.M., 3 P.M., or 9 P.M.). Arrange your main meals so that you allow 2 hours for digestion before exercising, or one hour after each snack.

DIETS FOR MAINTAINING WEIGHT OR LOSING WEIGHT GRADUALLY

We recommend the following pattern of eating for people interested in losing weight and for those who want to maintain their present weight. You can keep your weight down permanently if you continue to follow this new way of eating. In this system a person eats three meals a day. Each meal is lighter and smaller than the previous one. Breakfast is the main meal of the day. It gives you the major portion of your protein for the day and a great deal of energy too. Get up early enough so you can eat slowly until you are full. You should plan to have about half of your daily carbohydrates for breakfast and the remaining half for lunch and dinner. Here are two sample breakfast menus.

2 eggs (any style)
bacon, sausage, or ham (2 to 4 ounces)
1 small piece of fruit and 2 ounces cheese
1 piece of gluten toast with butter
1 cup of herb tea or decaffeinated coffee

or

1 portion meat, fish, or chicken
jacket of a baked potato (scrape the inside out until only ⅛ inch remains)
with butter or small amount sour cream
herb tea or decaffeinated coffee

Suppose you have overslept and you have no time to eat. There are still many ways to get a nutritious, high-protein meal. Have some leftovers—a chicken leg, a pork chop. How about a tuna salad (or any meat salad such as chicken or chopped liver) or hard-cooked eggs with a piece of cheese and fruit? Soft-boiled eggs only take 3 minutes and can be prepared in less time than it takes to dress. Some of these foods can be taken with you, eaten on the way to work, or when you arrive at work. Also available are canned meats such as ham, which can be sliced and eaten with no preparation. The choices are endless. We personally have made a complete meal of steak (broiled) and vegetables (steamed) with a piece of fruit and toast for breakfast when we felt like. It just takes a little organization and, of course, the desire to get a good start in the morning. But whatever you do, eat slowly, in as relaxed a setting as you can manage.

At your second meal, lunch (there are no snacks between meals), you will be eating one-half to two-thirds the amount you ate at the morning meal. This meal contains less protein and more low-carbohydrate vegetables. (You may wish to obtain a carbohydrate booklet for use as a guide.) Again, since you have eaten such a substantial meal in the morning, you may not be hungry, but do not skip your meals, because later you may become hungry and overeat. Some suggestions for this meal are as follows:

4 ounces tuna (water packed) or salmon (mix fish with 1 tablespoon of mayonnaise)
tomato, lettuce, and sprouts
low-calorie beverage

or

1 scoop of cottage cheese
½ tomato
¼ avocado
lettuce
low-calorie beverage

Whatever you choose for lunch, keep the amounts minimal. Eat only enough to satisfy your appetite, and be sure to get some protein in this meal.

Your evening meal should be eaten sometime before seven P.M. There is to be no food after seven P.M. Every evening meal consists of a very substantial salad containing almost no protein, no croutons or starchy vegetables or fruit. Walk through your local produce store and you will find many delicious additions to your salads. For example:

watercress	mustard greens	summer squash (crook-
Bibb lettuce	mushrooms	neck)
red lettuce	chives	zucchini
iceberg lettuce	scallions (green onions)	cauliflower
endive	red onions (sweet)	turnip greens
romaine	yellow onions	peppers (red or green,
escarole	radishes	hot or sweet)
spinach	carrots (grated, raw or	celery
parsley	cooked)	cucumbers
mint	asparagus	beets (grated)
beet greens	leeks	lemon rind (grated)
cabbage (red or green)	tomatoes	pimento
kale		

The combinations are endless and each will have a fresh crisp taste of its own.

As for a dressing for your salad—if you feel you need one, make your own. Here is a sugar-free recipe we use:

2 parts vinegar (your choice)
1 part olive oil
½ teaspoon dry mustard
¼ teaspoon black pepper
¼ teaspoon cayenne pepper
¼ teaspoon paprika
½ teaspoon caraway seeds
  Shake well and store in the refrigerator.

Avoid bottled dressings if possible; they almost always contain sugar, honey, or other high-calorie sweeteners.

If you have been eating in an irregular pattern, or eating light breakfasts and a large meal at night, it may take you a few weeks to adjust to your new eating style. We recommend that you stick with it for at least six weeks; we are sure you will then enjoy this pattern of eating. You will have more energy and your sleep will be sounder.

ALTERING YOUR EATING HABITS— THE FOOD JOURNAL

To experience faster and more satisfying steps toward your goal, we recommend altering your eating habits by changing the amounts you eat and times at which you eat. To become aware of your eating habits, keep a journal for at least four days. Continue to eat as you would normally, and write down the food, the amount, the time of day eaten and the reason for eating, and how the food tasted. Be sure to write down *everything* you eat, no matter how small the quantity. After four days, look at your journal. Do you eat your main meal at night? Do you eat between the three main meals? Do you eat after 7 P.M.? Do you feel stuffed after meals? Do you finish eating quickly? If you answer yes to any of these questions, we would suggest trying a change of eating habits.

Begin by setting aside a place in your home for eating. The dining-room table is the most logical place. Restrict all your eating to this area. If you must eat some of your meals out, avoid stand-up or quick food establishments. You want a place that is pleasant and will allow you to concentrate totally on your eating (no TV, reading, or other diversions at meal times). At all meals, remember to eat slowly and chew your food thoroughly.

The food journal will make you more conscious of your eating habits the longer you continue to keep it.

FOOD JOURNAL

Date	Food	Amount	Time of Day	Reason for Eating	Taste